T0139139

THE CYBERSECURITY SELF-HELP GUIDE

THE CYBERSECURITY SELF-HELP GUIDE

Arun Soni

CRC Press
Taylor & Francis Group
Boca Raton London New York

CRC Press is an imprint of the
Taylor & Francis Group, an **informa** business

First Edition published 2022
by CRC Press
6000 Broken Sound Parkway NW, Suite 300, Boca Raton, FL 33487-2742
and by CRC Press

2 Park Square, Milton Park, Abingdon, Oxon, OX14 4RN

ISBN: 978-0-367-70952-5 (hbk)
ISBN: 978-0-367-70953-2 (pbk)
ISBN: 978-1-003-14867-8 (ebk)

DOI: 10.1201/9781003148678

Typeset in Caslon
by KnowledgeWorks Global Ltd.

Contents

Preface

The Internet is a great tool for people and businesses because people can connect with the entire world and lookup for information. One can become "Global" from "Local" without any extra cost and within a few minutes.

Our involvement and dependence on technology are increasing day-by-day. In fact, in this pandemic, we have become 100% dependent on the Internet for every task, beginning from work to shopping, education, socializing and more. Never in history before people became so reliant on technology. Youngsters are becoming a soft target for threat actors as that segment uses the technology and the Internet most, that too without proper safety measures.

It is a worrisome situation that cybercrime is on the rise like never before. Email/Social media accounts hacking, Fake profiles, Spoofed emails, Phishing pages, Hidden cams, Unsecured Wi-Fi & routers, Online banking frauds, ATM frauds, Credit/Debit card frauds, Social networking sites dangers, Identity theft, Frauds through P2P money transfer apps, Romance scams, Revenge Porn, Cyberstalking etc. are creating havoc in personal lives.

There are books available that teach you ethical hacking. You need to have in-depth knowledge of Linux, Networking and many programming languages and databases to understand those. But there is a void of books for users who are not technical and are just acquainted with primary computer and Internet knowledge. They use technology and the Internet every day without any security measure and falling prey to threat actors. That is why cybercrime is rising exponentially due to the lack of awareness.

This book is an endeavour at the global level to impart online safety measures to all those people who want to secure themselves/their media and connected devices on the Internet.

The salient features of the book are:

1. The complete information is divided into multiple short chapters for easy understanding. Each chapter deals with a particular cyber threat and situation

2. Practical activities accompany each chapter to provide hands-on experience to readers.

3. The real-life scenarios and case studies at the beginning of each chapter bring readers nearer to understanding cyber threats. Now, they can relate to the topic more closely.

4. This book has a step-by-step graphical approach for a better understanding. We have tried to explain concepts with as many screenshots as possible to make understanding.

5. Many general topics like types of hackers and malware, Certifications in Cybersecurity and Careers in cybersecurity etc. been covered under the *"Must Read! Section."* Readers can read it even before starting to explore the book.

6. The last *"Explore it! Section"* consists of essential websites/extensions that can play a crucial role in your online safety. Our advice is to read each chapter and practice the practical part mentioned under the "Let's Do It!" section for complete learning. Also, do not forget to solve the Multiple Choice Questions to test yourself.

7. All trademarks, service marks, trade names, product names and logos appearing on images/screenshots are their respective owners' property.

8. All screenshots of various websites, apps and tools are being used by acquiring permission from respective copyright holders/developers. Also, all screenshots are as per guidelines laid down by various companies.

Happy reading....!

INTRODUCTION
THE WORLD OF CYBERCRIME

The World of Cybercrime

In the simplest definition, Cybercrime is a technology-assisted crime. It can involve PCs, smartphones, networks and the Internet.

Cybercrime is progressing at a breakneck pace, with constantly emerging new trends. Cybercriminals are becoming swifter, exploiting new technologies with lightning speed, tailoring their attacks using new methods, and coordinating with each other in ways we have not seen before. Since cybercriminals can operate remotely (maybe from a café or a beach), behind the veil of Internet anonymity, why one will take the risk of physically doing a robbery or theft?

If we take an example that if someone has to perform a theft, it is challenging because the ferocious dog, security guard, AI-enabled sensors, CCTV cameras, and many other security gadgets will be there around the intended house to protect it.

But, for a bad actor, it is easy to send a malicious link to the PC/smartphone of the victim. When the victim clicks on that link, some malware will get installed on the system of the victim, which will hack the device and compromise the banking/Credit card details. The anonymity of the Internet and borderless access provide additional security to cybercriminals. That is why Cybercrime is increasing exponentially without any statistics.

Before we start learning about Cybersecurity, it becomes necessary to know about various cyber crimes and their impact.

Understanding Various Types of Cybercrimes

There are too many cybercrime types, and each cybercriminal tries its best to use all kinds to victimize people.

Hacking

Hacking is an act committed by an invader by accessing your computer system without your permission. That invader can bypass/compromise the login details of your computer or any web account to access the victim's personal information. Even when you are typing a password/credit card number or any personal detail in an electronic device, and the person next to you can watch over your shoulder to get that information. It is termed "shoulder surfing."

Malware

Malware is some "malicious software" designed to gain access to or damage data in a computer. Malware can be of many types. All are deadly, and so we strictly need to have anti-malware software on our computers and smartphones too. Many times recovery is not possible once a victim's system got infected with it. Let us have a quick look at the typical type of malware.

Common types of malware include:

1. Viruses: these spread and corrupt data in a system.
2. Trojans: Trojan horse viruses (or simply Trojans) are disguised as legitimate software. These can create backdoors to let other malware enter into the victim's network. Through a backdoor, the attacker can access the infected system anytime and remotely.
3. Worms: these can infect all of the devices connected to a network
4. Ransomware: a ransomware encrypts a victim's data (holds your data hostage) until the victim pays money to the attacker. Still, there is no guarantee that the attacker will decrypt the files even after getting the money.
5. Botnets: it is a network of infected devices that work together under the control of an attacker.

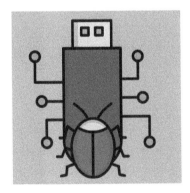

Spoofing

Spoofing is a type of cyber-attack in which someone attempts to disguise as a trusted source to have access to important information. Most of the spoofing happens through emails. For example, the victim might get an email from a local hospital in your area to register for the Covid vaccine. The scammer spoofed that email address to the local hospital's email address so that the victim believes the email is from the hospital. The information the victim enters through the reply of that email will go to that scammer.

Usually, the purpose of spoofing is to access personal information, bypass network security controls or to spread malware. Email spoofing, Caller-id spoofing, Website spoofing, IP address spoofing, DNS spoofing, and facial spoofing are examples of various kinds of spoofing.

Note: Facial spoofing is a type of spoofing that depends on facial recognition software to unlock devices or access a secure area. The photograph (or a 3D model) of the victim can compromise the facial recognition system if it is not built on advanced technology. Especially AI-based Deepfakes have made face spoofing a very convenient cyber attack.

Identity Theft

Identity theft occurs when some unauthorized person uses the victim's personally identifying information (PII), such as name, address, Social Security Number (SSN), credit card information, etc., to assume the victim's identity to commit some criminal act. For example, the bad actor can collect details about you from your social media accounts and get a mobile SIM issued fraudulently on your name.

Let us take one more example; Often, people do not collect their copy of the credit card receipt after making payment at restaurants/ supermarkets or elsewhere when they pay by credit card. The credit card number (or the last four digits of it) is printed on these receipts for anyone to see. With only this information, someone can make purchases online or by phone by linking more details of the victim to it.

Phishing

Phishing is a technique used by cybercriminals to extract confidential information such as credit card numbers and login details by impersonating themselves as legitimate entities.

Phishing is mainly carried out by email spoofing. You probably received an email containing links to legitimate appearing websites. When you click on such a link, the cloned/fake website opens, and whatever information you type is passed on to bad actors. That attacker can also install malware on your system through that website. Spear phishing is a targeted phishing attack. In spear phishing, emails are sent to just one person or organization.

Note: Vishing (voice phishing) involves calls to victims using a fake identity. It will fool the victim into considering the phone call to be from a trusted organization. Smishing is a form of Phishing that use SMS (texting) as a medium to trick users into clicking on a link.

Pharming

Pharming is a form of Phishing. Pharming is an attack that redirects your website traffic to another, probably a fictitious and malicious website. But, unlike Phishing, fake links are not used to trick a victim. Pharming is usually done by infecting DNS servers that are beyond control and remains undetectable. If your router is not secure, the bad actors can advantage of that to access the DNS settings and change those.

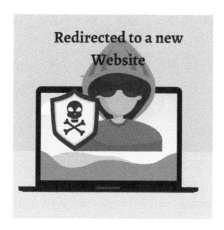

Note: The Domain Name System (DNS) is that part of the Internet, providing a way to match names (a website you're seeking) to numbers (the IP address for the website).

Web Jacking

Web jacking derives its name from "hijacking". Like hijackers take control of an airplane, here the hackers take control of the website and become the owner of the website. After taking control, they can modify the website. The original owner has no more control of the website. Sometimes the valuable information like a list of Client's is there, which can be used by attackers for any malicious purpose. The attackers can also ask for ransom or deface the website.

Cyberstalking/Cyberbullying

Like in physical stalking, the stalker stalks the person physically; in Cyberstalking, the person stalks the person virtually. With the proliferation of social media, virtual stalking has become easy. The stalker can easily follow the victim's movements as the victim himself/herself keeps updating the movement's status, like "watching the movie at PVR" or "Check-in at Singapore." A cyberstalker may be a stranger but could also be someone you know. Sending obscene, disturbing and demoralizing messages can affect the mental stage of the victim. These messages are sent using mediums like social media, SMS, and messaging services.

Note: cyberbully is usually referred to when a child or teen is involved, like the bully at school. Cyberstalking can happen between adults, and usually, a cyberstalker is obsessed with the victim with the perverse desire to control the victim.

A Denial-of-Service (DoS) Attack

A Denial-of-Service (DoS) attack attempts to deny service to intended users of that service. For example, a website becomes unaccessible because it got access requests (amount of traffic) beyond its capacity to handle. This type of attack takes advantage of the specific capacity limits applicable to any network resources and overloads the resources to break down.

Another variation of this attack is the DDoS attack Distributed Denial of Services (DDoS) attack. In a DDoS attack, multiple compromised computer systems attack a target, such as a server, website or other network resources, and cause a denial of service for users of the targeted resource. The multiple compromised systems can be anywhere geographically. The bad actor can operate these compromised systems without the knowledge and consent of the owner of these systems.

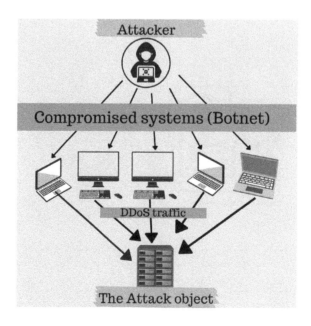

Social Engineering

It is the most dangerous attack and forms the basis of all types of cyberattacks. Social engineering is playing with the minds of people and taking advantage of the goodness of people.

Let us take an example. Your neighbor comes to your child, who is a teenager and very fond of playing online games. The neighbor gives him a smartphone and says, "I have bought this latest smartphone, and you can play any online game very smoothly. Connect it to your Wi-Fi and play that game. Your child takes that smartphone, connects to your Wi-Fi, plays the game and returns the phone. It seems all well and straightforward. But, what happened in-between was that the password of your Wi-Fi got stored in his smartphone. Now he can access the web through your Internet anytime. He used SOCIAL ENGINEERING to get the password of your Wi-Fi network.

While doing penetration testing of an organization, ethical hackers also test employees for social engineering and try to extract valuable information or login details from them

For a detailed introduction to the type of cybercrimes, follow this link: https://www.antifraudcentre-centreantifraude.ca/scams-fraudes/azindex-eng.htm

Shortened link for the same: http://bit.ly/cybercrime-types

Multiple Choice Questions

1. Which Cybercrime is related to the online bullying of the victim?
   a. Identity theft
   b. Phishing
   c. Cyberstalking
   d. Social Engineering

2. When an attacker sends an email to you and has your friend's name as the sender, it is an example of:
   a. Email spoofing
   b. SMS spoofing
   c. Facial spoofing
   d. Identity theft

3. This type of Cybercrime forms the basis of all kinds of cybercrimes:
   a. Identity theft
   b. Phishing
   c. Cyberstalking
   d. Social Engineering

4. This malware takes the victim's data hostage (encrypts) and releases it (decrypts) when the ransom amount is paid to the attacker:
   a. Virus
   b. Worm
   c. Trojan
   d. Ransomware

5. In which cyberattack, more than one compromised computers are involved in bringing down or crashing network resources/website/server?
   a. DoS
   b. DDoS
   c. SoDD
   d. None of the above

ANSWER KEY

1	2	3	4	5
c	a	d	d	b

1

ALL ABOUT IP ADDRESSES

Scenario

Have you ever wondered how devices' communication takes place in the Internet world? And, how your device has its own identity in this global network, making it different from the others? Many times you read that police has traced a cybercriminal. Do you wonder how cybercriminals get traced in this anonymous world of the Internet?

Objectives

- Concept of IP address and classification
- Step-by-step demonstration on how one can track an IP address

Introduction to IP Address

In the cyber world, you need an Internet address or an IP address to connect to others. In fact, the whole game of cybercrime and cybersecurity revolves around IP addresses. In this chapter, readers will learn about IP address and their types in detail.

The term IP Address stands for Internet Protocol Address, a unique number assigned to every user who uses the Internet. You can consider an IP address to be like a license plate on the motor vehicles, making one vehicle distinct from others.

In simpler terms, the IP address that one is using at a given time is their device's digital address, facilitating easy communication between devices.

DOI: 10.1201/9781003148678-2

About the Network Interface Card

To connect a computer to the Internet and other computers on a network, it must have a Network Interface Card (NIC) installed. The computers can then connect to routers, switches, or Wi-Fi networks and have their IP address provided by the Internet Service Provider (ISP). These days, almost all PCs come with NIC. You do not worry about adding anything extra to your device.

Note: If you are using a Desktop PC then connecting it to your Wi-Fi router wirelessly, you might need to have a USB Wi-Fi Adaptor.

Understanding Public and Private IP Addresses

The essential concept of IP addresses is public and private IP addresses.

Public IP

A public IP address is an IP address that is accessible through the Internet. We have no control over the IP as it is assigned by the Internet service provider when the device gets connected to the Internet. An example of a public IP is as below:

49.36.224.184

or

2405:101:1246: ddb6:29b1:76cc:6089

Private IP

Private internal addresses are only supposed to work within the local area network. These are not routed on the Internet, and no traffic can be sent to them from the Internet.

The routers that we have in our houses have the local IP addresses set to default by the manufacturer and are displayed to you. The IP addresses reserved for private IP depending on the size of the network are:

192.168.0.0 to 192.168.255.255 [65,536 IP addresses]
172.16.0.0 to 172.31.255.255 [1,048,576 IP addresses]
10.0.0.0 to 10.255.255.255 [16,777,216 IP addresses]

Network Address Translation

It is a process that involves your router to change your private IP address into a public IP address. That way, it can smoothly send your traffic to the Internet. It keeps track of the changes made in the process and operates on a router. An example of that is when you connect multiple devices on a network to the Internet with a single Internet connection. It is the NAT in-between, which is doing this task.

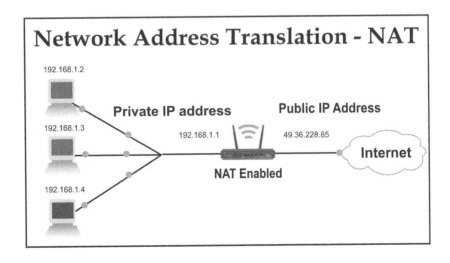

About Dynamic Host Configuration Protocol (DHCP)

DHCP stands for Dynamic Host Configuration Protocol. A DHCP server automatically assigns and centrally manages the IP address and other information to the clients in a network. On home networks, the ISP router usually provides the DHCP server. The IP address is leased to the device for a set period. When the duration is over, the IP address returns to the pool of available addresses unless the device renews the lease.

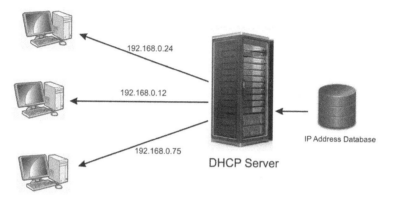

Note: The primary reason DHCP is needed is to simplify the management of IP addresses on networks by automatic management of IP addresses. That prevents duplicate IP address problems and minimizes configuration errors caused by manual IP address configuration.

Understanding IPv4 and IPv6 Addressing System

Let us understand the difference between IPv4 and IPv6 Addressing systems.

IPv4 Address

IPv4 is the 4th version of the internet protocol. It is the first version of internet protocol that has been widely deployed. IPv4 is a 32-bit number that is typically written in decimal digits.

For example, 49.36.28.105 is an IPv4 address.

The following are the significant parts of the IPv4 address.

Network Part

A unique number that is assigned to your network is considered as the network part.

Host Part

It is also a unique number that identifies the machine that is being used on the network. It is important to note that each host on a network has the same network part but a different host part.

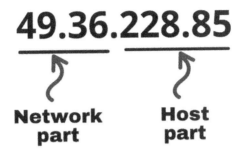

49.36.228.85

Network part   **Host part**

Note: When there are a large number of hosts on a particular network, then those hosts are divided into subnets, and the subnet number is assigned to each host.

- Networks are configured either manually or with DHCP
- It limits the Internet growth of existing users and also affects the use of the Internet for new users

IPv6 Address

The Internet will be able to grow to millions of times its current size using IPv6, in terms of the number of users, devices, and websites that form a part.

- IPv6 is the latest version of Internet Protocol. Unlike the IPv4, it has a size of 128-bits (16 bytes) which is why they have vastly enlarged addressed spaces.
- No more Network Address Translation (NAT) required. Also, it has auto configuration capabilities.

These look like:

201:5004:4050:2916:ee75:550c:8c5

128 bits

There is one further important classification of IP addresses, i.e., Static IP address and Dynamic IP address. But before beginning to learn about those, let us understand the concept of Domain Name System (DNS)

About the Domain Name System (DNS)

IP addresses are easy to remember and process for computers but challenging to remember by humans. DNS translates (or map) IP address to domain names. It allows internet users to access internet resources with ease. You can compare it with a phone directory in the smartphone where phone numbers are mapped to your contact names.

Note: Imagine every time you have to access google.com, you need to enter something like 142.250.72.206 in your address bar of your browser.

Understanding Static and Dynamic IP Addresses

There is one more important form of classification, which is Static and Dynamic IP addresses.

Static IP Address

A Static IP Address is a fixed address provided to the computer by the Internet Service Protocol (ISP). This number stays permanent unless the particular device is decommissioned or the network architecture changes. The advantages of using a Static IP Address are as follows:

- It provides the best DNS support.
- When Server Hosting, it becomes easier for customers to find you via DNS.
- It becomes easy to use Voice over Internet Protocol (VoIP) for teleconferencing or other voice and video communications.
- It becomes easier working remotely using a Virtual Private Network (VPN).

The disadvantages of using a Static IP Address are as follows:

- They are expensive because the ISP's charge extra, especially with consumer ISP plans.
- You are more vulnerable to hackers as they know exactly where your server is on the Internet.
- Anyone with proper network tools can easily find the person and its computer geolocation.

Dynamic IP Address

Dynamic addresses are used because the IPv4 may not be able to provide enough Static addresses.

A Dynamic IP Address is provided temporarily by your Internet Service Provider for a specific duration of time. They are assigned as needed by the DHCP (Dynamic Host Configuration Protocol) servers. The advantages of using a Dynamic IP Address are as follows:

- It has an easy and automatic configuration which means the DHCP server provides the next available IP address.
- It is practically cheaper than a Static IP address.

- It provides better internet security and makes it difficult for others to determine your device's exact location.

The disadvantages of using a Dynamic IP Address are as follows:

- It will not work well for hosted services like hosting websites or an email server.
- It limits remote access depending on your remote access software.
- It may have downtime and provides less-accurate geolocation.

Note: Downtime is the time during which a computer is unavailable for use.

Tracking an IP Address

Have you ever heard of being tracked by an IP address, which someone could have possibly extracted from an email? An ordinary citizen probably cannot locate your geographical co-ordinates but can tell about the region you are in and the service of which ISP you are using. The rest of the details (like your exact physical address) are with your ISP. The ISP hence maintains a complete record of all IP addresses mapped to a particular device and time. It is indeed possible to track and get tracked by an IP address.

Note: An IP address does not reveal personal information (like a name, social security number or house address). These details are provided only to legal authorities by the ISP.

Let's Do It! – Tracking Yourself

Here is a simple way to know your IP address with your geolocation and other details.

> **Step 1:** Open your web browser on your PC, and type the following URL:

https://whatismyipaddress.com/

Your IP address and other information will get displayed. To get more information, click on **Show Complete IP Details** link.

Let's Do It! – Tracking Someone Else from the IP Address

If you can capture the IP address of someone by some mean and want to know more about that person, follow the steps given:

1. Open your web browser on your PC, and type the following URL: https://www.whatismyipaddress.com.
2. Now click on the **IP Lookup** button.
3. In the text box, enter the IP address you want to look for and click on the "Lookup IP Address" button.

The details for that IP address will get displayed.

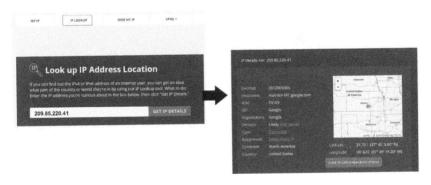

Similar Websites to Track IP Address

www.whatismyip.com
https://www.ip8.com/
https://www.ipapi.co/

Or

Type "What is my IP address" on Google search engine.

Conclusion

In this chapter, readers have been well acquainted with the concepts of IP addresses and their different types. The readers also understand how Network Address Translation (NAT) takes place and the idea of DHCP. The users even know how to find their public IP address and when they get hold of someone's IP address, then how to trace that person's location.

Multiple Choice Questions

1. Which system is concerned with changing an IP address to its equivalent domain name?
   a. DNS
   b. DHCP
   c. SND
   d. None of the above

2. Which system is responsible for automatically and dynamically allotting IP addresses to users?
   a. DNS
   b. DHCP
   c. DPCH
   d. None of the above

3. When you get connects to the Internet, you will get assigned with:
   a. Private IP
   b. Public IP
   c. DNS IP
   d. DHCP IP

4. Is it possible to track a user's region information from his public IP address?
   a. Yes
   b. No
   c. Sometimes
   d. I do not know

5. Which IP address is temporarily provided to you by your ISP and changes with time?
   a. Static IP
   b. Dynamic IP
   c. Private IP
   d. None of the above

ANSWER KEY

1	2	3	4	5
a	b	b	a	b

LAB TIME

1. Find your public IP
2. Find the details of IP address: 49.36.224.184
3. Explore the website www.ip8.com. What differences you find than www.whatismyipaddress.com?

2
ROUTER SECURITY

Scenario

It is a busy morning time. You have to use net banking to pay the electricity bill and check social media accounts to see what your friends have updated. While entering the net banking login details on your bank's website, just before clicking on the "Login to Net Banking" button, you realize it is a phishing website. Although you entered the correct URL of the website in the browser's address bar, its URL is different from the actual website. And, already, you had entered your login information in two social media accounts and now worried that those were also phishing pages. What happened overnight? Is my system hacked?

Yes, your router has been hacked.

Objectives

- The concept of a router and its types
- Understand the vulnerability of default passwords
- Checking and fixing the default password vulnerability practically

Introduction to Default Password Vulnerabilities

Nowadays, many people are being targeted to cyber-attacks, and routers are used as a medium of attack. The attackers exploit the vulnerability of default passwords (passwords provided by the manufacturer) or weak passwords of the routers to get into the network for their gain. Once the router gets compromised, every device connecting to it gets compromised.

As users, we must understand and learn different ways to check the routers' vulnerability and patch them up. Before starting, let us be clear about the concept of Modem and Router.

DOI: 10.1201/9781003148678-3

23

User name: admin

Password: admin

Modem

A modem is an acronym for "Modulator–Demodulator." It is a hardware component that allows a computer to connect to the Internet. It converts or "modulates" an analogue signal from a telephone line to digital data (1s and 0s) that a computer can recognize. Similarly, at the other end, it converts digital data from a computer into an analogue signal that can be sent over standard telephone lines.

Router

A router is a device that sets the communication between the Internet and the devices in your home. As its name implies, it "routes" traffic (data packets) between the devices and the Internet.

A Data Packet is a collective data unit made into a single packet sent over a network, either on LAN or the Internet. These packets have a source and destination IP address for the data to be transferred.

What Do We Have in Our Homes?

A modem is a box that connects a home computer to the Internet world. In contrast, a router is a box that allows the wired and wireless devices to use the Internet connection and allows them to talk to one another without having to do so over the Internet. Usually, an internet service provider will provide one single box that serves as both modem and router. It is evident that not all modems have routers included, and not all routers have modems present in them. For the devices in a home, there should be an integrated device for modem and routers. We will be referring to it as "Router."

Note: These routers operate using the Network Address Translation (NAT) technology. NAT technology helps several computers to connect to the wired router to share the same public IP address.

Types of Routers

The main three types of routers are as follows:

Wired Routers

Wired routers involve wired-cables that are used to connect directly to the computer. One connecting port on the router is used to communicate with the Internet while the others are used to connect directly with the computers to transfer data packets. Ethernet Broadband Router is one example of a wired router.

Wireless Routers

Unlike the wired routers, wireless routers have one connecting port that is connected to the modem. A wireless router known as a Wi-Fi router has one or many small antennas (antenna can be hidden inside the router's case) that help broadcast internet signals at home or office. The data packets are in binary code (series of 0's and 1's), which is further converted into radio signals. These radio signals are then broadcasted wirelessly via the antennae of the router. Its importance is that it allows users to have wireless access to the Internet.

Virtual Routers

A virtual router can provide a computer or server with the capabilities of a full-fledged router by using software to perform the router's network and packet routing functions. Virtual routing has various applications across many network domains, including data centre, cloud, branch, and service provider networks. But, It is still not considered a viable alternative to heavy-duty core IP routers, which assist in governing the Internet's core.

Note: These virtual routers are available for enterprises and not for home users.

Default Passwords

Every router has a username and password to access settings inside it. Default passwords are those passwords in a router that come with the product and are set by the manufacturer. Some of the default passwords set by famous router companies are (or look like) as shown in Figure on the next page.

Note: You can find default usernames and passwords for the router of any company and model from the website https://www.routerpasswords.com/

These default usernames and passwords are openly available on the Internet, and anyone can have access to those details. Your network administrator should make sure to change these default usernames and passwords at the time of installation. Otherwise, the attackers can access your routers from anywhere in the world and install malicious applications.

Note: One can access and change your router settings, including your Wi-Fi password and DNS settings. By changing the DNS

S. No.	Router	Username	Password
1	Belkin	admin	admin
2	BenQ	admin	Admin
3	D-Link	admin	Admin
4	Linksys	admin	Admin
5	Netgear	admin	password

settings, your Internet traffic can get directed to any phishing and malicious website. For example, you will type www.facebook.com, but presented with a phishing webpage, maybe www.faceb00k.com.

About Phishing Websites

Since we have started talking about phishing, do you know that about 70% of cybercrimes are done through phishing? Let us explore phishing in a bit more detail.

A phishing webpage is a replica of some official webpage. Threat actors use it to trick users into providing their personal information. Using these, they can capture login details to bank accounts, social networking sites and retrieve other sensitive information that can be used for malicious activity.

There are some ways in which a user can identify and protect him/her from phishing websites.

- Always check the URL of the website carefully. For example, an official website would represent www.Axisbank.com, while a phishing website might be www.Axxisbank.com or www.Axisbank1.com.

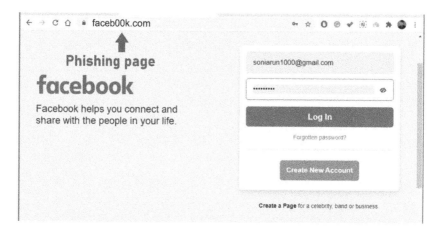

- Access the website by directly typing the URL in the address bar. A user may receive an email that may contain a URL or a link to the company website. Avoid clicking the link because you could become a victim of a phishing website.
- Keep an eye for the pop-up windows offering free antivirus software or scanning your computer that opens when you are accessing a website. It may indicate that the website is malicious.

Main Rules for Protecting a Wireless Router

A router can have many security flaws and can be hacked if necessary precautions are not taken beforehand. The following are some steps you can take to protect your router.

- Keep your router's firmware updated. Keep checking the router websites for any updates for the router.
- Always keep it password protected. The password should be complex.
- Change the SSID (service set identifier) from default to anything of your choice. For example, a default SSID like "Reliance Jio" will attract more bad actors than a new SSID like "Cyber surveillance team." An SSID is the name of your Wi-Fi, your router is broadcasting.
- Enable MAC address filtering by manually registering every device you want to use on the wireless connection to prevent others from joining the network.

- Make sure the firewall is enabled. It will protect it from being attacked by malicious websites.

Note: A firewall can be a piece of hardware or software that filters your network traffic and block outsiders from gaining unauthorized access to the data on your computer. A router's firewall can also protect all devices connected to it.

About Media Access Control Address (MAC)

Media Access Control (MAC) address is a unique hardware address that is assigned to a NIC (Network Interface Card). You can find the MAC address of your computer by going to the command prompt (by typing cmd in the search box of Windows 10) and typing ipconfig/all. The matter shown next to the field "Physical Address" is your MAC address. It will look something like: D0:0a:95:9d:68:16.

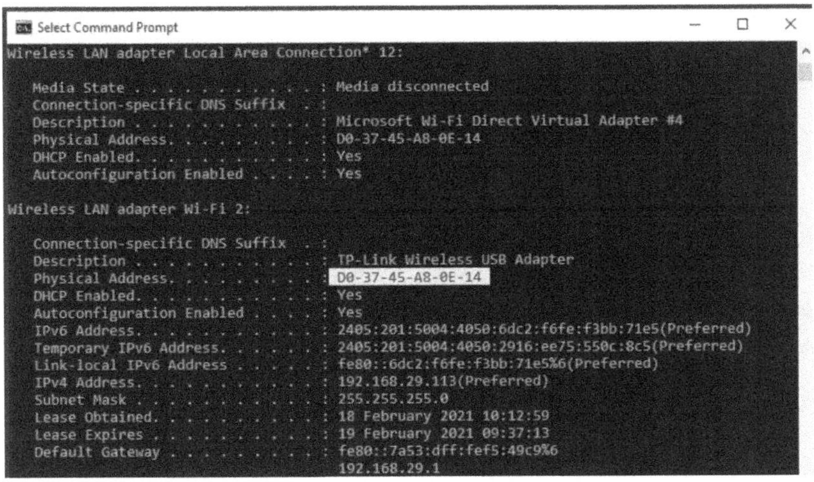

You can also find MAC address of your smartphone (here, Android ver 10) by going to Settings→About phone→Status information

Note: MAC addresses are usually assigned when the device is manufactured.

Methods to Keep Your Router Safe

We can take many steps to secure our router.

Updating the Router's Firmware

A router is a sort of gate that protects all of your devices connected to Wi-Fi from hackers. However, your router can't block new threats unless you keep its firmware updated. Here's the way to update your router to reinforce all of your devices' performance and improve your home security.

To update your router's firmware, follow the given steps:

1. Type your router's IP address into your browser's address bar and enter its login credentials to authenticate.
2. Locate the "Firmware" or "Router Upgrade" section and download the newest firmware update from your router manufacturer's website. Most probably, it will be a zip file. Unzip it into a folder.
3. Finally, through the Update section of your router, select that file and upload it to update the router's firmware and reboot the router.

Note: Do it carefully so that the upgrading process does not get interrupted. Otherwise, there could be irreversible damage to your router, so use extra caution.

Turning Off Unneeded Services

Many cyberattacks are a result of people taking advantage of security loop-holes or problems with these services. The number of unnecessary services that are running on the router should be disabled. Services like remote administration should be turned off if you are not required to access your router settings remotely. It will stop the access of bad actors to your router.

Setting Stronger Passwords

One should always make sure to set stronger passwords for the router, which cannot be easily guessed. Fulfil the following criteria for a strong password.

• It should have at least eight or more characters.
• It should be a combination of letters, numbers and a special character like! @ # and ?.

Let's Do It! – Checking the Router Security

Follow the steps given to check how secure your router is. We will try to access router settings through its admin panel

1. In Windows, at the command prompt, type **ipconfig** and press the Enter key.
2. In details, check the **Default gateway** and note down the IP address in front of it.

3. In the address bar of your browser, type that IP address. The router's authentication page will open.
4. Enter the user name as "admin" and password also as "admin." Again, if an error page is displayed, enter the username as "admin" and password as "password." If the router settings page opens, it means your router is unsafe. Otherwise, with an error page shown, it is safe.

Probing Further

1. Go to the website https://www.routerpasswords.com/. Select the make of your router. All the model numbers for that router company will be displayed. Check your router model number (which is generally written on the router and manual, which comes with it). Note down the default username and passwords for that.
2. Enter the same login credentials on the router's authentication page. In case an error page is displayed, then you are safe. If the settings page opens, it means your router is unsafe and can be hacked from anywhere in the world.

Remember that if you can open your router's settings page using the default username and password, anyone from anywhere can also do it. Many times default user name and passwords are displayed on the back of the router itself. You should always know about your router's user names and password and the method to change them.

Conclusion

Therefore, in this chapter, the readers have learnt about various types of routers. The default login credentials vulnerabilities can allow hackers to exploit and intrude into the network. The readers will now better understand how to keep their routers secure from password vulnerabilities and avoid being their devices getting compromised.

Multiple Choice Questions

1. Which attack is possible by compromising a router?
   a. DDoS attack
   b. Changing the DNS
   c. Wi-Fi hacking
   d. All of the above

2. The URL of a phishing page is:
   a. Same as of the original webpage
   b. Is always www.phishingpage.com
   c. Slightly different from the original webpage
   d. None of the above

3. What do you mean by Default Passwords?
   a. Passwords that your ISP changed
   b. Passwords set by the manufacturer
   c. Wi-Fi password
   d. All of the above

4. Which command do you type at the Window's command prompt to get your router's IP address?
   a. cmd
   b. ipconfig
   c. configip
   d. iconfig

5. Which is the correct way to restrict unauthorized access to your Wi-Fi as per this chapter?
   a. MAC filtering
   b. IP address filtering
   c. Never switch on your router
   d. None of the above

ANSWER KEY

1	2	3	4	5
d	c	b	b	a

LAB TIME

1. Check the security of your router against default login credentials.
2. Change the login credentials of your router.
3. Change your Wi-Fi password.
4. Change the SSID of your Wi-Fi.
5. Check the status of DNS in your router settings.
6. Check for the firewall settings in your router.

3

APPLYING 2-FACTOR AUTHENTICATION (2-FA)

Scenario

Just imagine you accessed your email and various social media accounts on a public computer (maybe in a library or cybercafé). After one day, all your contacts get messages on a social media platform on which you had an account (also from your email ID) that you need the money and send the money to this "xyz" account number. Your well-wishers started transferring money, and one also called you that which kind of emergency has happened. That is how you came to know that some bad actor has compromised your account. After analyzing the situation, you could deduce that you suffered this attack after accessing your accounts on that public computer.

Objectives

- Introduction to password capturing methods
- Importance of 2-FA
- Implementing practically 2-FA on your Gmail account

Introduction to Password Capturing

Emails and Social media has become an integral part of our lives now. As we get more Internet-savvy, we use and upload more and more information on social media platforms. Postal mail is almost dead and has been replaced by emails. Especially during the Covid-19 pandemic, the use of digital media has increased many-folds. For a second, think that someone has hacked your social media account and access/downloaded the emails/photographs/videos from your account is sufficient to give nightmares.

DOI: 10.1201/9781003148678-4

35

Our login credentials can be compromised in not maybe a dozen ways. Perhaps some bad actor could guess your password because it was weak (possibly your mobile number). Even if you had a strong password, the computer you used in a cybercafé had a keylogger (software that records keystrokes) to capture username and password. The situation is alarming!

Before proceeding further, we must know the ways our password or login details can get captured.

Password Capturing Methods

There are many ways login credentials can be compromised. If we know a few of them, then you can protect yourself against those.

Weak Passwords

If you have your password as your mobile number, date of birth, your spouse name, 123456, I love you etc., consider it hacked within a few seconds only by guessing, without using any tool.

Dictionary Attack

In a Dictionary attack, all words in a dictionary (or number sequence) are tried against your password. Suppose there is a word that you used as a password, your digital identity will get compromised. That is why we recommend that you do not use a dictionary word as a password. It is also possible that in a dictionary attack, an attacker uses a so-called "word list," much like a writer would use a dictionary.

Brute Force Attack

This type of attack is very sharp and has a high success rate. In this type of attack, almost all combinations of keys on your keyboard are tried against your password. There is a very high possibility that there will be one combination which is your password. Since lots of per-mutation and combinations of keyboard characters are formed, this attack is very time-consuming. So long and complex the password, better are chances of delaying/defeating the attack.

Keylogger

These are software which, when once installed, can record whatever you type on a computer. These are just not restricted to recording keystrokes. High-end keyloggers can record keystrokes, screenshots of websites you access, your voice through mike available with your PC/Smartphone, your recording through the webcam. There are also hardware keyloggers that sit between the keyboard connecting port and the keyboard cable. No antivirus can detect these.

Phishing Pages

Phishing is a type of online scam where cybercriminals impersonate legitimate organizations via email, text message, and web pages to steal sensitive information.

A phishing web page is a replica of an original web page. It is devel-oped to compromise one's login details. For example, when you use a public computer, you find the Facebook page or Gmail page already opened. If that is a phishing page, the login details which you enter will get captured. Remember that the only difference between an original web page and a phishing web page is the URL. A phishing web page of Facebook can have a URL www.facelook.com or www.faceb00k.com. So always check the URL before entering the login details.

Note: It is advised that you use a passphrase instead of a password. A passphrase can be a sentence and has spaces in-between the words. For example, I AM a Good Boy is a passphrase.

How to Defeat All These Attacks?

Suppose still, after all precautions, somehow your login details get captured. In that case, there is 2-FA (or also called Multi-Factor Authentication), which can protect you. When implemented, you can defeat all attempts to take control of your account by a bad actor; even your login details are in his possession.

What Is 2-FA

In 2-FA, you link your mobile phone with your email account or social media account. After entering the username and password, you will get a verification code on your mobile phone when you log in. Along with the password, you need to enter that verification code in the provided space. Only after doing this, your account will open.

1. The first factor is the password
2. The second factor is the verification code

You can now analyze that even when someone gets your login details, the person can still not access your account. It is because the verification code will come only on your Smartphone. Hence, your account is safe.

Let's Do It! – Applying 2-FA to Your Gmail Account

1. Log-in to your Gmail account. Click on your profile image. Select the **Manage your Google Account** option.
2. Select the **Security** option from the left tab. On the right-hand side, under the **Signing to Google section** in front of **2-Step Verification**, click on the **Off** option.

3. The 2-step verification process will start. Click on **Get Started**.
4. Verify your identity by login into your account and click on the **Next** button.

5. Select the Device you want to link and click on **Continue.**
6. The next step is important as it will provide you with a verification code on your mobile phone. Enter your mobile number and click on **Send.** Google will send a verification code to your selected mobile number.

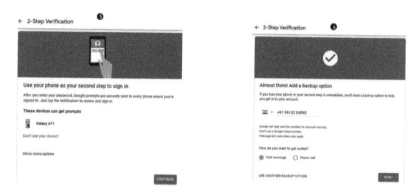

7. You will be prompted to enter the code.
8. Enter that code on the screen in the space provided. Click on **Next.**

9. Finally, you will be asked to turn on the 2-Step Verification option. Click on **Turn ON**. Now the 2-FA will get applied. The Google Prompt will be the default method for 2-FA.

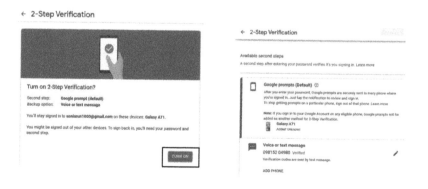

10. On this screen, when you scroll down, you will get the option to get back up codes.

These backup codes help you access your account when you do not have your Smartphone with you and still want to access your Gmail account.

Note: Look for the "Trusted Device" option and enable/disable it as required.

Google Prompt Method

You can also use the sign-in with Google prompts. This is the default method of sign-in. It is easier to tap a prompt than enter a verification code. Moreover, prompts can also help protect against SIM swap and other phone number-based hacks.

Google prompts are actually notifications you will receive when:

- You have Android phones signed in to your Google account.
- You have iPhones with the Gmail app and signed in to your Google account.

Based on the notification, you can:

- Allow the sign-in if you requested it by tapping **Yes.**
- Block the sign-in if you didn't request it by tapping **No.**
- For added security, Google may ask you for your PIN or other confirmation.

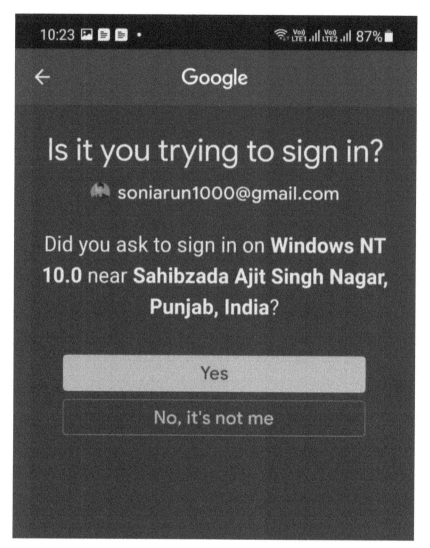

This prompt is the second step of verification

Verifying

Open the incognito mode (private window) and try to login with your Gmail account. You will get a prompt as shown in the above Figure.

Note: When you apply 2-FA to email accounts from other email/ social media account providers, you might get some verification code on your mobile number. It depends on the "provider" how it deals with the second factor.

Setting Up 2-FA for Your WhatsApp Account

When you set 2-FA for your WhatsApp account, you will have to input a PIN that only you know whenever you are re-registering your phone number with WhatsApp. In other words, if you (or someone else) are trying to associate a new device with your phone number, it will be impossible as they require your PIN to finish the setup process along with the registration code that gets texted to a phone number. If you forget the PIN, WhatsApp can email it to you as you need to associate an email account while implementing 2-FA. WhatsApp will keep reminding you to enter the PIN at random intervals of days. For implementing 2-FA in your WhatsApp account, follow the steps: **Settings→Account→Two-step verification**.

Note: You can also add a fingerprint lock for another extra layer of security by following the **Settings→Account→Privacy→Fingerprint lock** sequence of steps.

Conclusion

Here readers understood various types of password cracking attacks, leading to your email/social media account's hacking. Some methods are difficult to defeat (like brute-force attack or keyloggers). The only protection we can have for our online accounts is by implementing 2-FA.

Multiple Choice Questions

1. What do you call a duplicate page of an original page of a reputed company (but having a different URL), which someone develops to capture your login credentials?
   a. Fishing pages
   b. Duplicate pages
   c. Phishing pages
   d. Keylogging page

2. Which type of password attack is the slowest but most effective?
   a. Dictionary attack
   b. Brute-password attack
   c. Weak password attack
   d. None of the above

3. Which software can record your keystrokes when you type anything from your keyboard?
   a. Keylogger
   b. Loggerkey
   c. Locklogger
   d. None of the above

4. If you have to capture someone's username and password by recording keystrokes, which method will you prefer to employ?
   a. Dictionary attack
   b. Brute-password attack
   c. Phishing attack
   d. Keylogger attack

5. 2-Step Verification is also known as:
   a. 2-FA
   b. Multi-Factor Authentication
   c. a and b
   d. Uni-factor security

ANSWER KEY

1	2	3	4	5
c	b	a	d	c

LAB TIME

1. Do the following:
   a. Implement 2-Step Verification to your email account you operate.
   b. Try to log in from a different device and see how it works.
2. Implement 2-Step Verification to all your social media accounts.
3. For your WhatsApp account:
   a. Implement 2-FA
   b. Implement Fingerprint security

4
HAS MY EMAIL
BEEN HACKED?

Scenario 1

Suddenly you got suspicious that somebody is reading your confidential emails and even sending emails from your email account. You came to know about it because you saw an email in the Sent folder which you did not send to your contacts. You think that somebody has got the log-in details of your email account. What to do now?

Scenario 2

You went on a trip to Singapore and used the hotel's business center to access your email account. After coming back to your country, you realized that you just closed the window without signing out of your email account. Now, you are worried that someone there might be reading your emails. What to do now?

Objectives

- To know has your Gmail being accessed secretly by anyone
- Find out from which devices you have been logged-in
- Secure your Gmail in-case you find something suspicious
- Track who accessed your Gmail in an unauthorized way

Introduction to Log-in Activities

You may have used your email account at a computer of cybercafé/ business center or any public computer and forgot to sign off. Now, you are worried. Well, there is a way to overcome this situation.

DOI: 10.1201/9781003148678-5   **47**

These days many email providers like Gmail, Yahoo, and Outlook. com provide you with a feature, which will enable you to track the recent log-in activities for your email account. You can monitor activities like different logged-in locations/devices, the IP address from where the account was accessed, and also the time it was accessed through this feature.

Moreover, at the same time, you can also sign-out from all suspicious logged-in devices. Since Gmail is the most used email provider these days, we will take an example of a Gmail account.

Let's do it! To check is anybody accessing your Gmail account in an unauthorized manner.

1. Log-in to your Gmail account
2. Scroll down to the right bottom of the screen
3. Click on **Details** option

An **Activity information** page opens with a listing of recent logged-in activities related to your email account. Now you can see all details and can have an idea that if you did not access your account at some particular time, it means someone has unauthorized access.

Note: Now, you have the IP address of the person who accessed your account without your permission, you can go to www.whatismyipaddress.com and check out his details

For getting a closer look, and when you want to sign out from a particular device or location (in-case you forgot to sign off earlier from another computer), click on the **Security Checkup** option.

4. The **Security Checkup** page opens.

   a. Click on the down arrowhead in front of the **Your Devices** option.

   b. You will get a list of devices from where you are currently logged-in. Click on three dots in front of the device from which you want to sign out. Click on the **Sign out** option. You will be signed out from that particular device.

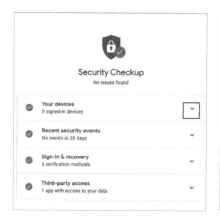

c. In case you want to be more secure, change your Gmail account's password by clicking on the **Don't recognize this device?**

Follow the given steps:

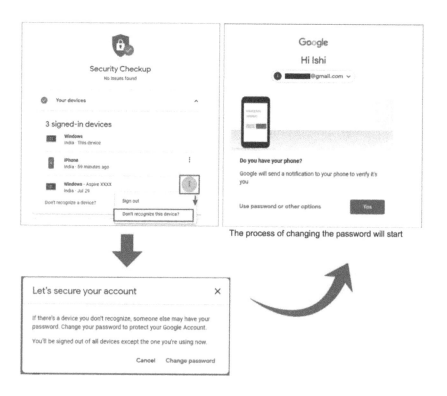

Note: While changing the password, if you choose the method to verify through your phone, keep your phone with you, as you will get a verification code on that. If you select a way to send the verification code on your recovery email id, keep log-in details of that email id with you.

Remove Third-Party Access

Many times, Google lets you allow third-party apps and services access to different parts of your Google Account like Google Drive and Google Calendar. These companies are neither developed nor owned by Google. You should check and stop unnecessary companies from accessing your data.

1. Select **Third-party access** (refer to first figure on page 50)
2. Select the app or service you want to remove
3. Select **Remove Access**

In the Case of Hotmail/Outlook.com Service Provider

If you have an account on outlook.com (old Hotmail.com), then follow the steps given:

1. Click on your profile image and click on the **My account** option.
2. In the Privacy box, click on the **Activity History** option.
3. Click on the Security tab in the Sign-in Activity box. Click on the **View my activity** option.
4. You will see the log-in activity of your account.

You can observe that all email service providers have different methods to show your email account's recent activities. But we recommend Gmail, as it has a straightforward way to access and an easy-to-understand interface of current log-in activities.

Note: In outlook.com, the main thing to observe, there is no sign-out option from a particular device. So in case you monitor any unusual activity, you are required to change the password to secure your account.

Conclusion

It is an excellent way to secure yourself by checking your recent log-in activities (from where you are logged-in). Almost all reputed email providers and various social media platforms provide this feature. Try to explore this feature in social media platforms; it is mainly available under Settings→Security. All online platforms keep changing names of terms and positioning of elements. So the screenshots may vary the time readers perform these steps.

Multiple Choice Questions

1. On which link did you click in Gmail account to get recent log-in details?
   a. Recent
   b. Details
   c. Log-in activities
   d. None of the above.

2. How many recent log-in activities get displayed when you clicked on the Details link in the inbox of your Gmail account?
   a. 9
   b. 4
   c. 5
   d. 10

3. Which is the most appropriate action to take when you see many unauthorized recent log-in activities from various multiple unknown devices?
   a. Stop using that email account
   b. Log-out from all devices one-by-one
   c. Change your password
   d. Start crying

4. Is it possible to check that the recent log-in activity was from a smartphone or a PC?
   a. Yes
   b. No
   c. Sometimes
   d. I do not know

5. In a Gmail account, on which links do you click to check sign-in from various devices?
   a. Security Checkup→Your Devices
   b. Details→ Sign-in & Recovery
   c. Security Checkup→Third party access
   d. Details→Your Devices

ANSWER KEY

1	2	3	4	5
b	d	c	a	a

LAB TIME

1. In your email account, review the recent log-in activities.
2. Suppose there is a provision in your email account to log-out from a particular/all devices.
   a. Log-out from a particular device and check recent log-in activities.
   b. Re-login from that device and again check recent log-in activities.
   c. If that option is not there, change the account password to secure your email account.
3. Create a sample email account, on any email provider and attach a recovery email account and your mobile number with it. Change password of your email account using:
   a. the recovery email
   b. using your Smartphone

5
IMPLEMENTING ONLINE PARENTAL CONTROL

Scenario

Suddenly you find out that your child who just entered his/her teens has withdrawn from the real world. He/she is not eating usual, talking less and is showing signs of depression. You tried to talk to the child but failed. Most of the time, your child is with the smartphone. Then one day, when he/she left the smartphone unattended, you saw some push notifications threatening your child on the pretext of some issue. You also get terrified now. What to do? Of course, you will take the help of the cybercrime cell. But you regret that you should have monitored your young child's activities.

Overview

- Threats posed on the Internet for children due to digital transformation
- To set up parental control for the children to create safe searches, monitor children's online activity and install parental control on the DNS level

Introduction to Cyber Threats to Children

The pandemic has transformed the world entirely by bringing a drastic shift from classroom teaching to online classes. This sudden shift was implemented at the beginning of the year, leaving various countries to conduct regular studies using a virtual medium.

In this digital transformation age, it has been a nightmare for parents to keep their children away from the predators waiting for them on the Internet. The children have been spending long hours of their day before the computers and smartphones, which could have been in control of bad actors.

DOI: 10.1201/9781003148678-6

Cyber offenders and strangers have found that young children and teenagers are perfect targets for criminal acts. As they are often trusting, naive, curious, adventuresome and looking forward to attention and affection. Today, the danger to children is even more significant because of digital transformation, and the web provides anonymity to such predators. Whether the victimization occurs face to face or over the Internet, the method is the same. The perpetrator uses the details about the child to focus on a child victim. For instance, the predator may initiate a web friendship with a young person, sharing hobbies and interests. This might cause the exchange of gifts and pictures (even objectionable ones).

Some of the online threats for children are listed below:

Child Pornography

This has become a rising concern where young children are being lured into the heinous acts of child pornography. There are reports that children as young as seven years were sending their objectionable photographs to strangers on their directions during their online classes.

Cyberstalking

The reckless usage of children's social networking websites can also lead to stalking on the virtual platform by people with wrong intentions.

Cyberbullying

In children, it has become prevalent these days due to the pattern of online schooling. Cyberbullying refers to harassment, threatening, and making others do things against their wishes through some online platform.

Hacking

Children spending a lot of time on the Internet has given the hackers just new bait for their attacks. The information about themselves or their family, which they spread online inadvertently, can cause a lot of harm.

Note: Many times, downloading malicious and not age-appropriate apps on Smartphones result in these conditions.

Parental Controls

Parental controls are a set of software or options provided in devices and systems which allow parents to monitor their child's Internet activity. Parental controls can prevent children from accessing inappropriate or indecent content online. The parental control feature can

- Block or have control over the type of video games played by children (or suggested to them).
- Create filters for the usage of websites and use only the websites approved by the parents.
- Stop the children from using a website that the parent not preferred or has content related to drugs/alcohol, suicide and pornography.
- What exactly are your children looking at online, and who's targeting content at them? You can also control their screen time.
- Control the mobile apps which they download on the smartphone.

Note: While using parental control apps for monitoring your child, take care of your country's rules and regulations related to the child's age.

Here are three measures we are suggesting to have parental control in your house.

Google Safe Search

A safe search tends to prevent pornography and offensive content from showing in search results. It is pretty easy to activate the safe search feature present in the Google search engine. Here are steps you would like to require to put in a secure search on your web browsers. To turn on the Safe Search, follow the given steps:

1. Open the Google search engine, https://www.google.com/ preferences.
2. Under the Safe Search Filters, enable the Checkbox "Turn on SafeSearch."

Note: Although you can turn on the Safe search, there is still the possibility that it will not prevent objectionable contents with 100% accuracy.

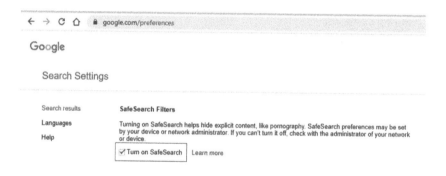

Google Family Link App for Parents

The Google Family Link app allows parents to set digital ground rules to guide their young ones when they are active online. Advantages of Google Family Link for Parents:

- It helps in setting daily screen time limits for the child's device
- It sets a bedtime for the device
- Parents can track the child's location
- It can remotely lock the child's device
- It helps in managing the applications used by the child
- Parents can approve or block apps the child wants to get from the Google Play Store.

- Parents can keep a tab on how much time their child spends on any particular application.

Let's Do It! – Steps to Set Up Google Family Link for Parents

1. Go to the Google Playstore and download **Google Family Link for parents** app.
2. Continue as a parent and start setting up the application.
3. Link the child's device with the code provided on the parent device by following the next step.
4. Now you need to have your child's smartphone and download the **Google Family Link for children & teenagers** app. In that, enter the code shown on your (parent) phone in your child's phone when prompted. Your child's phone will get connected to your phone. In the same manner, you can create a network with your children and can control their activities.

Note: Do read FAQ https://families.google.com/familylink/faq/ about the Google Family Link app. You can also manage your child's access to websites when using the Chrome browser on their Android or Chrome OS device.

Device Compatibility

There could be some compatibility issues while downloading this app on Android and iOS devices.

For Kids and Teens

Family Link runs on Android devices running version 7 and higher. Devices running Android versions 5.0 and 6.0 (Lollipop and Marshmallow) may also be able to run Family Link.

For Parents

Parents can run Family Link on Android devices running versions 5.0 (Lollipop) and higher and iPhones running iOS 11 and higher.

Some other similar apps:

1. Net nanny
2. Bark
3. Kaspersky Safe kids

Note: All of these apps are paid but not expensive. These can protect your child from inappropriate content like Violence, Bullying, Drugs/alcohol, Self-harm/Suicide and sensual content. Moreover, nothing is more expensive than the mental health of your child.

Changing DNS in Your Router

It is the hardware route to secure your devices. Domain Name System (DNS) is like a database consisting of the Website address (URL) and corresponding IP address. Many companies are providing family-friendly DNS servers. Apply those DNS servers so that no objectionable website opens in any device connected to the Internet through your router.

One such company is Open DNS Family Shield, and DNS servers are:

- Primary DNS server: 208.67.222.222
- Secondary DNS Server: 208.67.220.22

Let's Do It! – Steps to Add These DNS Servers to Your Router

1. Open the login panel of your router in the web browser by entering its private IP in the address bar and entering the login credentials.
2. Go to DNS Settings and change the DNS settings to above provided DNS servers. Click on the Save option.
3. Exit and reboot the router.

Now your home network, which is through that router, becomes completely secure, and no device connected to it (with wires or wirelessly) can open any non-friendly website.

Note: We hope you remember that you can find your router's IP address. It is by typing **ipconfig** at the command prompt of your Windows OS. The IP address next to the **Default gateway** is the IP address of your router.

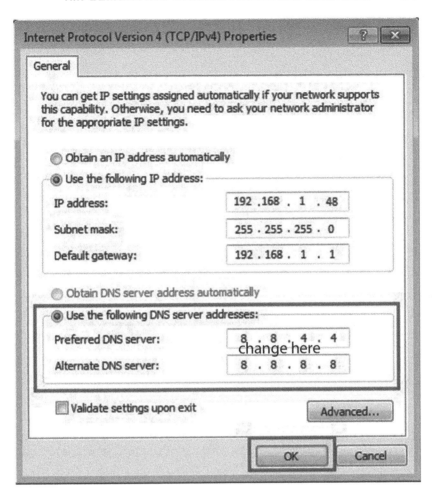

More Companies That Provide Family-Friendly DNS Servers

CleanBrowsing

- Primary DNS server: 185.228.168.168
- Secondary DNS Server: 185.228.169.168

SafeSurfer

- Primary DNS server: 104.197.28.121
- Secondary DNS Server: 104.155.237.225

DNS for Family

- Primary DNS server: 94.130.180.225
- Secondary DNS Server: 78.47.64.161

In different routers, this option can vary in its position. Usually, you will find it under Network→LAN settings. There is also a **Content Filtering** option available under the **Security** section in most of the routers. One can use the **Blocked Keywords** option and **Approved URLs** option by turning it ON. One can make use of these for strict safe parenting.

Conclusion

Hence, in this chapter, readers have understood the threats that children might face in the cyber world. To relieve the parents' worry, they have been introduced to the parental control concept and methods. Now they know the various types of parental control methods to monitor their children's online activity. Make sure you check your country's rules to monitor your children.

Multiple Choice Questions

1. The term used to harassing someone using social media is called:
   a. Hacking
   b. Cyberbullying
   c. Social engineering
   d. None of the above

2. While using the Google family link app, do you also need your child's device?
   a. Yes
   b. No
   c. Sometimes
   d. I am not concerned

3. Which other app is like the Google family link app?
   a. Net Nanny
   b. CleanBrowsing
   c. Tree
   d. SafeSurfer

4. Which command will help to find the default gateway (private IP of your router)?
   a. Lpconfig
   b. Ipconfig
   c. Configip
   d. pconfig

5. When you give **ipconfig** command to check the private IP address of the router, it will be displayed against this term?
   a. Fixed gateway
   b. Default gateway
   c. Subnet mask
   d. IPv4 address

ANSWER KEY

1	2	3	4	5
b	a	a	b	b

LAB TIME

1. Open your router settings by entering your router login credentials.
   i. Check the default DNS server assigned and note it down
   ii. Exit the settings
   iii. Reboot the router
2. Use Google to find more companies that provide free family safe DNS server IPs.
   a. Change the default DNS servers with the family safe DNS servers in your router and reboot the router.
   b. Also, set Safe Search in the Google search engine

6

THE GOLDEN RULE TO BE ON SOCIAL MEDIA

Scenario

You just saw one of your photographs, which you uploaded on a social media platform, sent to you on your WhatsApp by some unknown person in a morphed form. You are scared now. The person can blackmail you directly on this pretext. He can also send it to your contacts, and it will be difficult for you to explain to everyone that this is a morphed image of you.

Objectives

- Learn about watermark to safeguard image/video on social media
- Applying watermarks on photographs/videos on a PC
- Watermarking pictures on your phone using an app

Introduction to Watermarking

These days, this situation has become a common phenomenon for such acts. The images/videos can be morphed quickly by threat actors by using Artificial intelligence-powered tools. AI is becoming cheaper, and AI models are getting well-trained day-by-day because lots of data is available now. So it has become essential to safeguard whatever (images, videos and PDFs) you post online. As there are around 200 popular social media platforms, it is almost impossible to monitor and & implement the security to every social media platform you use. There must be one golden rule to safeguard your contents.

DOI: 10.1201/9781003148678-7

What Is a Watermark?

A watermark can be a symbol, name, signature, shape, or even QR code superimposed on a media with a controlled transparency level. If your contents are watermarked, then if somebody tries to produce them as their own, the watermark will prove that the contents originally belong to someone else. That is why you are advised to display a logo, shape, signature, your name or a message as a watermark on contents. You can watermark all your documents, including PDFs, video, and photographs, before uploading on a social media website and even before sending it to someone.

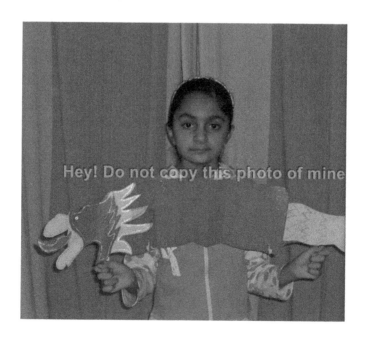

Note: Even if someone takes a screenshot of contents, the watermark will go along.

Remember that the placement, size, and transparency matters for your watermark. A vague and small watermark applied on a corner of an image can easily be removed or cropped. It would help if you had a big enough watermark, transparency up to 50%, and placed prominently in the middle of the image. So, when someone tries to remove it from your contents, the person cannot do without changing the actual contents.

Many free software and smartphone apps are available to apply watermark on content (especially on images and videos). These are powerful software that can get an entire folder of photographs watermarked within seconds. You do not need to watermark each picture individually.

Suppose you do not find enough features in free software or smartphone app to have full control over watermarking. In that case, you can always buy one as these are not expensive.

We will be using the **uMark** software downloaded from www. uconomix.com in the Let's do it! section. It is powerful software, and using it; you can easily add watermarks to images, videos, and PDFs. The following screenshot appears after downloading the uMark software and before executing it.

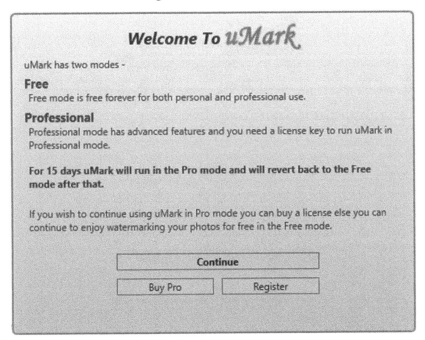

You can see that this software is free to use for the first 15 days, and after that, you can buy it if required. If your requirement is not much, you can always use the free version, which comes with some limitations. Some advanced features like watermarking unlimited batch of images in one go, watermark tiling, output file renaming, output file resizing, save watermarks for repeated use, generate thumbnails, and custom quality jpeg images are not available in the free version. But for an average user (unless you are a celebrity) free version is sufficient.

Let's Do It! – Downloading and Using uMark Software

1. Download the uMark software from www.uconomix.com as per your operating system. Install it by executing the downloaded file.
2. Open the **File** menu and select the **Add Images** option.

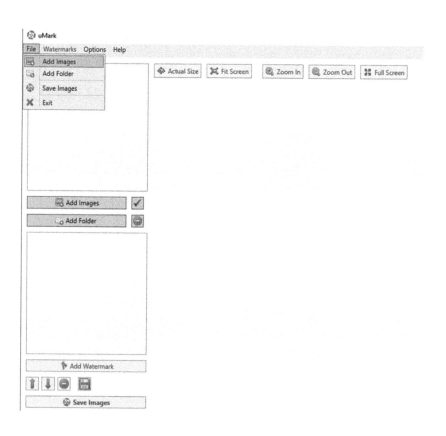

3. Select the image to which you want to add a watermark.

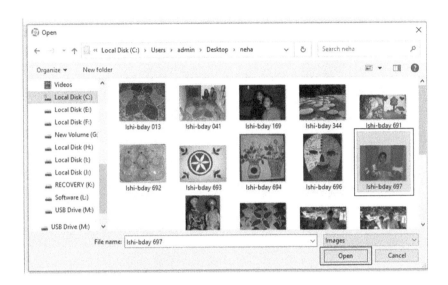

4. The image will open. Click on **Add Watermark** button and select the type of watermark you want to add (here, we are choosing the **Add Text Watermark** option).

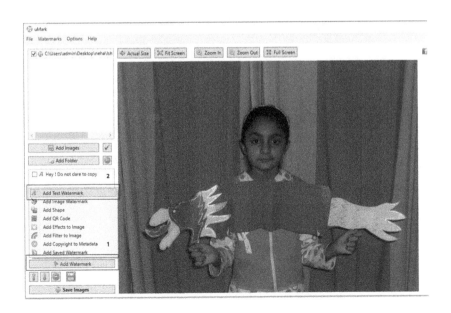

5. The **Watermarking Settings** dialog box opens. Type the text which you want to add as a watermark. Give the required effects and specify its position. Click on the **Ok** button.

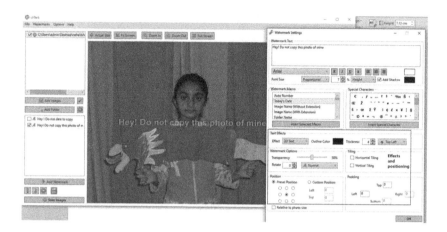

... The watermark will get added.

Note: QR code is a great way to add as a watermark. You can create a free QR code from a website like https://www.qrcode-monkey.com/ or https://www.the-qrcode-generator.com/, which can redirect users to your blog or website on scanning the code. Then add this QR code as the watermark. This will secure your image as well as direct the users to your blog/website.

Some Other Websites for Watermarking

https://www.batchwatermark.com/ is a great website that is completely free for adding text or an image as a watermark on your images. There is nothing to install, and 100% free forever.

https://pixiko.com/ is a nice site to add watermark to your videos.

https://www.kapwing.com/ is another great website to add watermark to your videos.

Android apps for watermarking

1. Photo watermark
   • Link: http://bit.ly/photowatermark
2. LogoLicious
   • Link: http://bit.ly/logolicious

3. Add Watermark on Photos
- Link: http://bit.ly/addwatermark2

iOS apps for watermarking

1. LogoLicious
- Link: http://bit.ly/logolicious2
2. eZY Watermark
- Link: http://bit.ly/ezy10

Conclusion

It is great to be on social media. But some threat actors can always misuse your photographs/videos. Morphed/altered images and videos have become an everyday norm. Since it is not easy to monitor where the image is being misused, we can say that watermarking can prove a golden rule to protect our online media.

Multiple Choice Questions

1. Which is the correct placement of the watermark in a photograph?
   a. In the right corner
   b. In the left corner
   c. In the center
   d. At the bottom

2. Which of the following website provides 100% free watermarking forever?
   a. Watermarkingbatch.com
   b. Batchwatermarking.com
   c. uMark.com
   d. None of the above

3. Which of the following is a wrong statement?
   a. Watermarking spoils the face beauty in a photograph
   b. Watermarking is an effective way to safeguard your online media
   c. For effective watermarking, you need to have the correct placement
   d. None of the above

4. Which one is not an app for watermarking?
   a. Watermark photo
   b. Photo watermark
   c. LogoLicious
   d. eZY Watermark

5. What extra benefit you will get when you watermark your content with a QR code?
   a. You can direct the user to Google
   b. You can direct the user to your personal blog/website
   c. You can hack a user's phone
   d. None of the above

ANSWER KEY

1	2	3	4	5
c	b	a	a	b

LAB TIME

1. Add multiple images to a folder, whom you want to watermark. Add a watermark to all images in the folder in one go. See which tool/website/app does that best.
2. Generate a QR code that directs you to www.arunsoni.in and add it as a watermark on your photograph.
3. Use the kapwing website to add a watermark to one of your videos.

7

SMARTPHONE SECURITY/
FINDING YOUR LOST PHONE

Scenario

You just bought a brand new phone. After downloading all the essential apps, it is time to set a screen lock. But you get confused because there were so many options available, and you do not know which one you should prefer? Is pattern lock better or a four-digit pin? Is the Face recognition method better than the fingerprint scanner? And, among this confusion, you might end up setting a weak security lock.

Many times, our smartphone gets misplaced or stolen. You become afraid as many personal pictures and videos were inside, which could be misused. The situation is horrible.

Objectives

- Concept of smartphone security and the types of threats that are posed due to low protection
- Various methods of authentications of smartphones to keep them secure
- How to track the stolen or misplaced smartphone?

Introduction to Smartphone Security

Personal data that is stored on one's phone is worth so much that it can be considered priceless. It means that a user can never afford to get compromised with the security of his phone.

There is a considerable risk involved in smartphones as there is always the possibility of information being leaked. We will be learning about the security and tracking of smartphones as an individual.

DOI: 10.1201/9781003148678-8

Smartphone Security

Adding a screen lock to the smartphone prohibits access to crucial banking apps, emails, social media platforms and other data. It is usually simple to adjust to the smartphones' lock screen settings to construct a strong barrier between the outside world network and the phone.

Some of the users tend to have low smartphone configuration of specific parameters, leading to security breaches. An attacker or a hacker can target the victim's smartphone through various ways like:

- Phishing Attack
- Data leakage or Data Loss due to weak screen lock
- Malware Attack

Authentication in Smartphones

As smartphones are advancing day by day, security concerns are also rising. It is one reason that various methods have been developed to keep smartphones secured from multiple types of threats. The different types of authentications that are present in smartphones are as follow:

Passwords

They are the simplest form of authentication measure that is used as a form of smartphone security. If a password is well thought of, it can be considered safe to use. Otherwise, using a weak password (like your dog's name) can be guessed easily.

PIN Number

A PIN is usually like a password but generally in a numerical form. The PINs can be of 4-Digit, 6-Digit, or even 16-Digit PIN in a smartphone. It could be an unsecured authentication method if a simple PIN is kept by the smartphone user, making the smartphone vulnerable to various threats.

Pattern Lock

These authentication methods unlock the phone only when the correct pattern is input on a square box with a 3 x 3 grid. Many people tend to select the most commonly used shape, which becomes a security risk for smartphone users. It is considered one of the most accessible methods of authentication for a smartphone user.

Fingerprint Scanner

It is one of the most preferred methods of authentication in smartphones. It is considered one of the most secure forms of authentication, but then it has its own weakness as the fingerprint scanner is not always convenient and can refuse to work with a dirty or wet finger.

Facial Recognition

It is again one of the trending authentication methods as it is effortless to use. But the widespread use of face unlocking without adequate hardware will always result in lower security for modern smartphones. It can also not rely on a trusted method of authentication for essential things like financial transactions.

Tracking Your Phone

Most Android phones now come with a built-in **Find My Device** feature. This service automatically tracks your phone's location. Use this service on an Android phone by enabling the **Find My Mobile**

option in your phone's **Biometrics and Security** Settings. Similarly, the iPhone also has the **Find My iPhone** feature.

Note: The option name can vary depending on the Android and iOS version you are using.

Let's Do It! – Tracking Your Missing Android Phone

To locate an Android phone, follow the given steps:

1. Pick up a PC or a smartphone of your friend, log in to your same Gmail account with which you were logged-in to your Android phone.
2. In the address bar of your browser, enter **google.com/android/find**. The location of your phone will be displayed on Google map with the following three options:
   a. **Play Sound**: You can play a sound so that it makes noise (even if you had put it on silent mode).
   b. **Secure Device**: You can secure your device so that the finder can't access your home screen. This feature is most helpful if your phone wasn't previously secured with a screen lock.
   c. **Erase Device**: You can erase your phone. It is the best option if you know for sure that you aren't likely to retrieve your phone. Remember that after erasing, you will not be able to track it.
3. If you are just interested in finding the exact location of your phone, follow the given steps:
   a. Click on the Green phone location icon

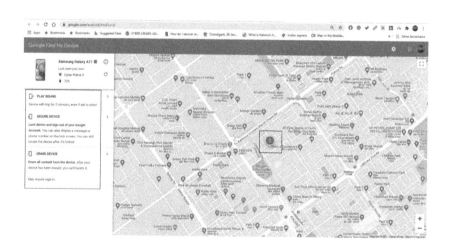

b. On the leftmost corner, you will see three horizontal lines. Click on that, and a menu will open. Click on the **Your Timeline** option.

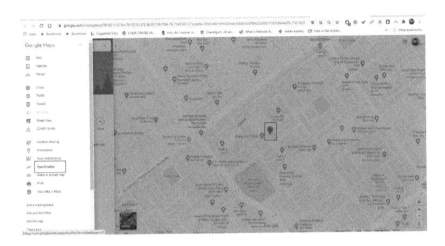

c. You will see the location timeline and places you have visited in the previous six months. Click on the **Today** button. You can see the last location. It is there where your phone is.

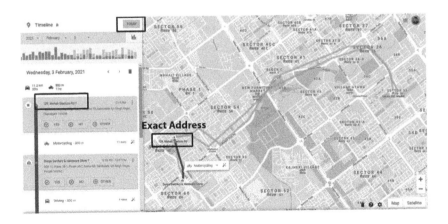

Note: You can also type "Android Device manager" or "Where is my phone" in the Google search engine to find your phone's location on the Google map.

Let's Do It! – Tracking Your Missing iPhone

To locate an iPhone or iPad, follow the given steps:

1. On your PC, open the website www.icloud.com and login with your iCloud credentials.
2. Click on the **Find iPhone** icon.
3. The location of your device will be visible on the Map. You can see that there are three options:
   a. **Play Sound:** The sound will start playing on your device. This option is generally useful when your phone is around, but you cannot trace it.
   b. **Lost Mode:** Follow the onscreen steps. You can display a phone number on the missing device's screen to whom the finder can call. You can also enter a custom message asking the finder of your lost device to contact you. Click on **Done**. The phone will get locked with the passcode keeping your information secured.
   c. **Erase iPhone:** To prevent anyone else from accessing the data on your missing device, you can erase it remotely. Remember that when you erase your device, all of your information (including credit, debit or pre-paid cards for Apple Pay) is deleted from the device. Remember that after you erase a device, you can't track it.

Note: Given the amount of sensitive personal information that we keep on our mobile devices these days, including banking details, encrypting your device is a very sensible decision. These days both Android and iOS phones with the latest versions of OS (In Android ver 10 and onwards) come with default encryption ON. For older devices, you need to research how to encrypt the data and do it carefully. Also, do not forget to take cloud data backup regularly as these electronic devices can fail to boot with any unfortunate incident.

Conclusion

After reading this chapter, the readers are now aware of the concept of smartphone security, the potential threats, the methods of authentication to be used as a lock to secure the smartphone from attackers. Also, a misplaced phone can be easily tracked by a phone's inbuilt features, provided you know how to do it.

Multiple Choice Questions

1. Which screen lock type you consider the safest for your smartphone?
   a. PIN code
   b. Facial recognition
   c. Pattern
   d. Fingerprint scanning

2. Which PIN do you consider secured?
   a. 1234
   b. 2468
   c. 0000
   d. 8346

3. Suppose you have lost your Android phone in your home somewhere. Which option will be suitable to find it?
   a. Erase Device
   b. Secure Device
   c. Play Sound
   d. None of the above

4. Suppose you just realized that you had lost your Android phone in the market somewhere. Which option will be suitable to find it?
   a. Erase Device
   b. Secure Device
   c. Play Sound
   d. Tell mom

5. Suppose you lost your Android phone in the market a week back and cannot find it. In that case which option will be suitable?
   a. Erase Device
   b. Secure Device
   c. Play Sound
   d. Tell dad

ANSWER KEY

1	2	3	4	5
d	d	c	b	a

LAB TIME

1. Put your phone in silent mode and then play sound through another device.
2. Consider your device lost. Secure it (do not try the Erase option).

8

ALL ABOUT PROXY AND VPN

Scenario

Suppose Bob is living in a country with multiple restrictions on the web. He wants to access some widely available content on some other country's server. How can he do this, sitting in his country? Also, he wants to access free Wi-Fi provided by the hotel where he is staying and is afraid that someone will eavesdrop on the communication. What is the solution?

Objectives

After studying this unit, the reader should be able to:

- Difference between Proxy and VPN
- Step-by-step method to create your very own Virtual Private Network in Windows system

Introduction to Anonymity

There are times in our lives where we come before situations where we want to anonymously surf the Internet by hiding or changing our IP address, or if we want to access something on the Internet that is not available on our region's server due to multiple reasons like geo-blocking or content filtering.

Sometimes we also fear sending confidential information or type our credentials over the Internet. We are afraid that someone could be capturing your network packets and want an encrypted transfer of data for the same.

Proxy

A proxy is defined as a service that operates as a gateway between you and your Internet traffic. Your activities appear as if they are from somewhere else.

DOI: 10.1201/9781003148678-9

83

Though the proxies can conceal your IP address, one of its most significant downsides is not providing encrypted services. If an unauthorized person is eavesdropping, your message will be displayed in plain text format. To get proper control over your Internet privacy, use a VPN as the service.

VPN

VPN stands for Virtual Private Network, which functions like proxies but has a tunnel for encrypted transfer of data, enhancing the privacy and security of the user surfing the Internet. They are one of the best options which can let one access websites and applications that are region- restricted.

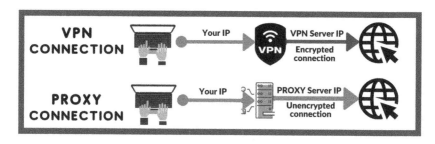

Note: VPN and proxies both hide the IP address, but the only VPN encrypts data and provides Operating System-level security.

The VPN encapsulates the data packets, verifies user credentials, and then provides an encrypted tunnel to send the message; the request is sent to the desired server. Then that server will decrypt the message and hence, forward it to the Internet. As soon as you get your requested data, it will be encrypted by the VPN server and delivered back to you.

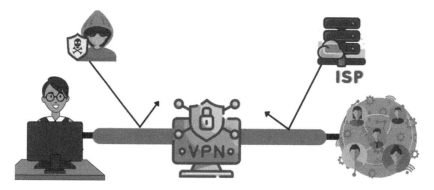

To provide a secure connection, VPN works on the following most widely used protocols:

- Point-To-Point Transfer Protocol (PPTP)
- Open VPN
- Layer Two Tunneling Protocol (L2TP)
- Secure Sockets Layer/Transport Layer Security Protocol (SSL/TLS)
- IP security (IPsec)

Note: PPTP is a high-speed VPN protocol. It is effortless to set up and configure on most of the operating systems and devices. Due to the protocol's high cross-platform compatibility rate, a PPTP connection can be established on multiple platforms. But there is a downside too. A PPTP connection can be blocked quite easily by firewalls. If your data is very confidential, then think of Open VPN or other protocols, which cannot be blocked, and provide better encryption.

Pros and Cons of Using a VPN

There are both pros and cons of using a VPN

Pros of Using a VPN

1. *Bypass Geo-restrictions on websites and contents:* An individual can access contents and websites regardless of his geolocation. If a website or content is blocked in a particular country, an individual can easily access those using a VPN.
2. *Anonymity:* A VPN encrypts your data and keeps your private information safe. It restricts hackers, ISP or government officials from snooping around your personal information.

Cons of Using a VPN

1. *Compromises with Internet speed:* Using Free VPN services may slow down your connection speed, maybe by just a few Mbps.
2. *Threats from Anti-VPN software:* Some websites or streaming services may try to combat VPN connections using

VPN blockers to ensure the content is not accessible to everyone. It is essential to choose a reliable VPN to avoid such situations.

Setting Up a VPN in an Android Smartphone

A quick guide to set up a VPN on an Android smartphone

Let's Do It! – Getting a VPN on Your Android Phone

Step 1: Install Atlas VPN (free VPN) from Google Play Store on your android phone or https://atlasvpn.com/vpn-for-android.

Step 2: After it gets installed, open the application, and you will be prompted to accept the terms and conditions.

Step 3: A new connection request prompt will open. Click on the **Ok** button.

Step 4: A list of servers of various countries will be displayed (to have availability for more countries, you can buy a premium subscription).

Step 5: Now, when you surf the Internet, you can see that it shows the server's results of the country you have selected.

Setting Up a Personal VPN in a Windows 10 PC

For a quick, anonymous and secure browser, you can create your browser in Windows 10. VPN Book attempts to keep the Internet safe and free by providing free and secure PPTP and Open VPN service access for everyone. PPTP Stands for "Point-to-Point Tunneling Protocol." PPTP is a networking standard for connecting to virtual private networks.

Let's Do It! – A Quick Guide to Setting Up a VPN in a Windows 10 PC

Do the following on your PC having Windows 10:

1. Open settings in your Windows PC and click on **Network & Internet** Option.

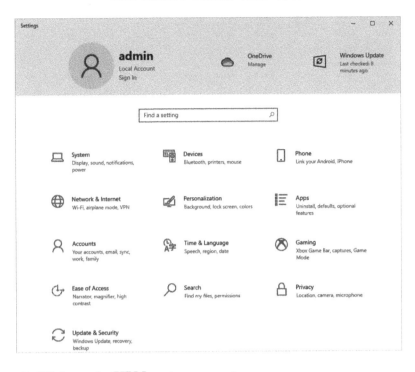

2. Click on the **VPN** option to continue

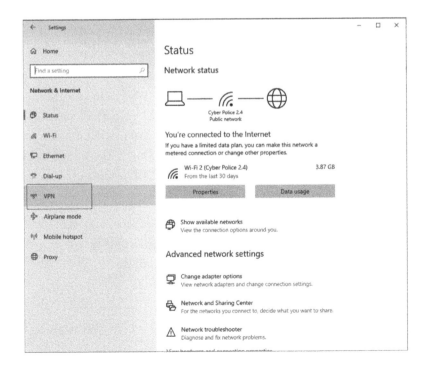

3. Click on **+ Add a VPN** Connection option

4. Now open your web browser and type "VPN book," and from the first link you get, click on "VPN Book." VPN Book has one such PPTP VPN that works without any installation. It can be set up on windows PC by just adding the link to the server and using the sign-in details. Click on the **PPTP** option.

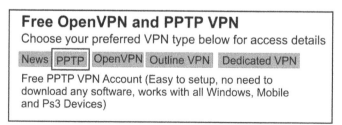

5. Select and copy the country's link from which you want to belong after connecting to the VPN. Also, note down the username and password.

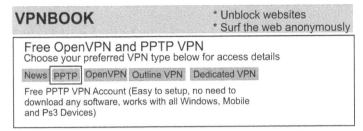

VPNBOOK

* Unblock websites
* Surf the web anonymously

Free OpenVPN and PPTP VPN
Choose your preferred VPN type below for access details

News | PPTP | OpenVPN | Outline VPN | Dedicated VPN

Free PPTP VPN Account (Easy to setup, no need to
download any software, works with all Windows, Mobile
and Ps3 Devices)

- Poland VPN Server:pl226.vpnbook.com
- Germany VPN Server:de4.vpnbook.com
- Following servers are optimized for fast web surfing:no p2p downloading
- US VPN Server:us1.vpnbook.com
- US VPN Server:us2.vpnbook.com
- France VPN Server:fr1.vpnbook.com
- Canada VPN Server:ca222.vpnbook.com ◀━
- Canada VPN Server:ca198.vpnbook.com

Username:vpnbook

Password:mku97sb

More servers are coming

* This service is Advertisement and Donation based, if you enjoy this service, please consider donating
so we can keep this as a free service and add more servers in the future.

6. Add the VPN provider, which is built-in windows settings,
type the connection name, and paste the preferred server
name. As in the VPN Book, the sign-in info is using username and password; type the mentioned username and password and click on the **Save** button to continue.

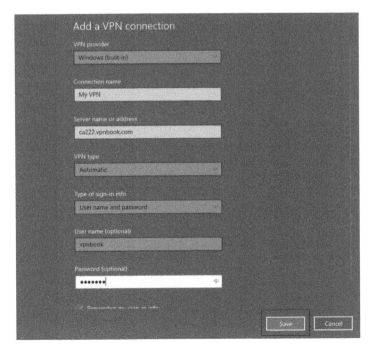

7. Now, you can see the VPN is set up, and you are ready to surf the Internet freely and securely by clicking on the **Connect** button.

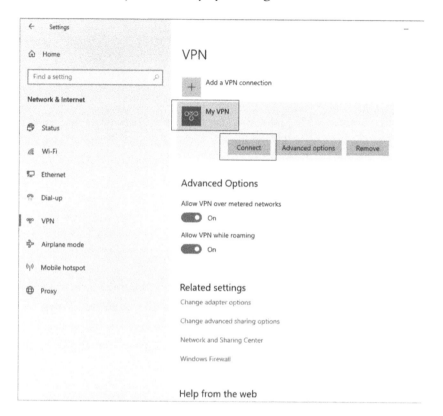

8. You can check that you are connecting to the VPN you have created.

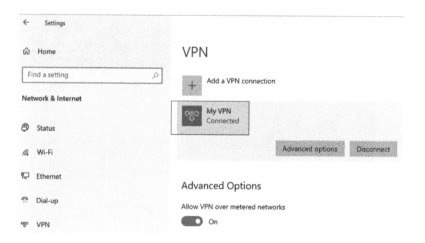

9. To ensure that your VPN is active, go to www.whatismyip. com and see your current IP details.

My IP Information

My Public IPv4 Is: 192.99.37.222
Your IPv6 is: Not Detected

My IP Location Info ❓	My IP Hostname
City: Beauharnois	ISP: OVH Hosting Inc.
State: Quebec	Host Name: ns513859.ip-192-99-37.net
Country: Canada	16276
Postal Code: J6N 0A2	
Time Zone: -05:00	

Port Scanner   Hide My IP   IP Blacklist Check   Speed Test

You can see that your IP address has changed according to the server you have chosen (in our case, it was Canada).

Link to Other Similar VPN

The following VPN are paid VPN, which you can purchase for additional security features. These are compatible with Android, Windows, and iOS devices. You can use the trial which some of these VPN providers provide. If satisfied, then purchase the VPN premium version to use all the VPN features and have the highest secure connection.

Express VPN: https://www.expressvpn.com/
Nord VPN: https://www.nordvpn.com/
Ghost VPN: https://www.cyberghostvpn.com/

Note: Most of the paid VPNs also have a kill switch. It means that you will be automatically disconnected from the Internet if the VPN stops working for some reason.

Some Points to Consider before Selecting a VPN

Before selecting a VPN you can consider the following points:

- While free VPNs are appealing, we do not recommend using them. Even if you don't pay for it with money, you will pay for it in some other way, whether it's through advertisements, poor streaming quality or unreliable protection.
- Choose a VPN which support strictly No Logs policy. It means they do not keep track of your personal information, where you go online, what you download, or what you search for.
- Look for a VPN service that operates inside or near to your country. This way, you can address many speed-related issues with virtual private networks by ensuring that information must not travel long distances to reach its server.
- The total number of servers that a VPN company operates directly impacts how much traffic it can handle, so look for a virtual private network with as many servers as possible. The better equipped a service is to manage traffic, the faster traffic can move.
- VPNs change all the time. So prefer VPNs that offer 24 × 7 live chat because emails and tickets can take hours to answer.
- Some VPNs do not support all platforms. Make sure that the VPN you choose supports major platforms like Windows, Mac, Android, Linux, and iOS.

Conclusion

Here readers have understood the difference between the usage of proxies and VPN. They have also understood the advantages and disadvantages of a VPN. The setup of a VPN in the Windows system has been demonstrated step-by-step.

Multiple Choice Questions

1. Which one hides your actual IP address but do not provide encryption to the data?
   a. Proxy
   b. VPN
   c. NPP
   d. None of the above

2. Which one is more secure?
   a. Proxy
   b. VPN
   c. Both provide the same level of security
   d. I don't know

3. Which is not a VPN protocol?
   a. PPTP
   b. OpenVPN
   c. Layer Two Tunneling Protocol (L2TP)
   d. SecIP

4. Which is the most secured VPN protocol?
   a. PPTP
   b. OpenVPN
   c. Layer Two Tunneling Protocol (L2TP)
   d. SecIP

5. In this chapter, you have learnt to create a self VPN of which protocol?
   a. PPTP
   b. OpenVPN
   c. Layer Two Tunneling Protocol (L2TP)
   d. IPSec

ANSWER KEY

1	2	3	4	5
a	b	d	b	a

LAB TIME

1. Find free VPN apps on your Smartphone.
2. Use a VPN on your phone.
3. Create a VPN for your windows system using a France server.

9

COLLECTING THE
DIGITAL EVIDENCE

Scenario

You were browsing the Internet, and suddenly a pop-up opens in your browser where you see your morphed image in an objectionable form. Or somebody sends you a link, and when you click on that link, a web-page opens where you see your video in an offensive altered form. You suddenly realize that somebody has downloaded images and videos from your favorite social media platform and altered those. But now the disaster has been done, and it is time to respond. If you want to complain against the offender and bring him to the court of law, you need to file a complaint against him with a digital proof of his wrongdoing.

Overview

- Importance of Digital Evidence
- Collecting an email header as digital evidence
- Producing a long web page as a single image as a digital evidence
- Having a long web page or altered video to collect as digital evidence in the form of a video
- Producing a WhatsApp Chat as a digital evidence

Introduction to Importance of Digital Evidence

Now, this is the time that you should do some disaster management. You need to collect the evidence to be attached as proof with the complaint that you will register with your area's cyber cell. Now you have to address two issues:

1. It would be best if you do it immediately. Suppose you are waiting for the professional digital forensic team to come and collect it as digital evidence and in that case, the offender may have deleted the morphed image/video/fake profile.

2. You must collect the digital evidence such that it does not change anything in the captured evidence. Like it should not change the date stamp. For example, when a file has been created, the date and the time of creation get attached to it. But if you modify it even after adding a dot and save it again, its date and time will change.

Note: For an abusive comment or a message sent on any messaging app, take a screenshot of that. You can do it by pressing the Print Screen key and paste it into a document (could be a paint or a word file and then save the file) on a PC. It would be best if you have learnt how to capture the screenshot on a smartphone, as different makes and models have different methods to capture the screenshot.

We will consider here two cases:

1. Someone has sent you an objectionable email. You want to attach it as digital evidence along with your complaint letter.
2. You saw your morphed or altered images on a website and the web page that could be 20 screens long. How to save the complete webpage as a single screenshot or create a video of that lengthy webpage?

Let's Do It! – Producing an Email/Web Page/Video as Digital Evidence

Each email received has a header. Email headers contain essential information. That can include the name of the sender and receiver, the path (servers and other devices) through which the message has traversed, and many different types of information.

Typically email headers can provide data such as:

1. Who sent and received the email
2. The entire network path the email has passed through

3. Timestamp information

4. Information about the email client used

5. Information about the device used

Email forensic analysis is used to determine the source and content of the email message as evidence. It identifies the actual sender, the recipient and the date and time it was sent, etc., to collect reliable evidence to bring criminals to justice.

Case I: When you receive an email, just taking the message's screenshot is not sufficient. You need to know how to probe further. Follow the steps given for producing a received email as Digital evidence.

Since Gmail is the most used email provider, we are considering that in our example.

1. Open the received email from the inbox. Click on the three vertical dots and select the **Show original** option.

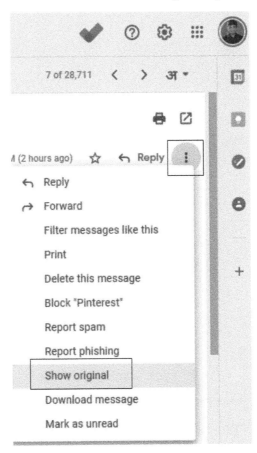

2. The following screen appears. The section under Original message gives a lot of information. Click on the **Copy to Clipboard** button. Open a new MS Word file and select the **Paste** option. It will paste the clipboard content in the Word file

3. The pasted content will look something like this:

```
Delivered-To: soniarun1000@gmail.com
Received: by 2002:a05:7110:6406:b029:2b:b4c8:94f4 with SMTP id a6csp569845@gee;
    Tue, 22 Dec 2020 15:23:03 -0800 (PST)
X-Google-Smtp-Source: ABdhPJykn2qpsgWd77rVsr578i5iOLMxyg3WO+3+AVTD2x7KmiEGKk6tuMbXOpaIpxqImuq3aru10
X-Received: by 2002:a92:ba42:: with SMTP id o63mr23396397i11.93.1608679383598;
    Tue, 22 Dec 2020 15:23:03 -0800 (PST)
ARC-Seal: i=1; a=rsa-sha256; t=1608679383; cv=none;
    d=google.com; s=arc-20160816;
    b=8Tgs573mUQ+d7ZQlwq4UCko4PlWzfa5muUNm/fdz6CTkMd4qwFQaNplAFKvru2/Ru5
    2GrAhgp0bQaJkctglR2p1DXsiKgD9Twrd5gEUMqNLLE3x31Fugjy0wMeR7vkTks9N5mr
    11F86F0TJGnXL34v2HhsO3mPHKOG0maEph3ZXmilGxsp3OOu3y2r8Ihpa4PwpFTL6YHN
    1QIEZ1zCcOOhPOQKh0ciwnbABa5fkNmPB6f1455tNXNdKa2kt13m6p5bDBIqfTECJqH1
    v3f9sTN3sj2pAQEK5SMpu6VLllhghZ7namuogpbBJhKzEgaGb+BVaGGRtC/tbnfgQrw7
    LVQwv+
ARC-Message-Signature: i=1; a=rsa-sha256; c=relaxed/relaxed; d=google.com; s=arc-20160816;
    h=content-transfer-encoding:mime-version:feedback-id:to:reply-to
    :message-id:subject:date:from:dkim-signature:dkim-signature;
    bh=YDSGV+tUI9uEjnAoqC24Re0Qu+iYx9b28n6HJrmQ7Du=;
    b=x3J+0Q/nOkeb93GaqMF720srv3pDCez6/peSJm9Ft0iNaOQGJNRagx/xmLTi+ZagA5
    qnCW6FG5IzsAR2xmOmCnVelR7xfT4CHFn4PF4Z85JKghRQDMzKy1umagMPxtmll6aSqp3
    GDIwzKvPgYLBoSPby7YHsa2c4w7JhTxDeHXWdlFA/wwqjrz874CWI0vJgFUH+cgpO4ah/z
    hLVBMBUHhIo/BFEb3aj1coEUaFt5xF+ygfBwyeyEcvap/tP9/Vs1MLwD51xDXD+SkevG
    f6U81Al#J4QkNLhy02mOUMR1PI+MVC01GAv7YXxeMU1kY6sd5nxU+lF/r/HFydggiRDFy
    MKpA+=
ARC-Authentication-Results: i=1; mx.google.com;
    dkim=pass header.i=@applytojob.com header.s=2017112912073pm header.b=lYcuzHd0;
    dkim=pass header.i=@pm.mtasv.net header.s=pm header.b=OSODtACR;
    spf=pass (google.com: domain of pm_bounces@pm-bounces.applytojob.com designates 104.245.209.211 as permitted sender) smtp.mailfrom=pm_bounces@pm-
bounces.applytojob.com;
    dmarc=pass (p=NONE sp=NONE dis=NONE) header.from=applytojob.com
Return-Path: <pm_bounces@pm-bounces.applytojob.com>
Received: from mta211a-ord.mtasv.net (mta211a-ord.mtasv.net. [104.245.209.211])
    by mx.google.com with ESMTPS id n13s1122255641oh.4.2020.12.22.15.23.03
    for <soniarun1000@gmail.com>
    (version=TLS1_2 cipher=ECDHE-ECDSA-AES128-GCM-SHA256 bits=128/128);
    Tue, 22 Dec 2020 15:23:03 -0800 (PST)
```

Digital forensic experts can analyze this to get the required information.

Case II: We have to capture a long web page (maybe 20 screens long). Taking a screenshot of each screen and then joining them can harm the evidence. There is one Nimbus extension for Chrome browser that you can install. Using that, you can capture a long web page as a single screenshot or create a video of that and do much more. You can also capture recording of a video which you want to produce as digital evidence.

1. Open your Chrome browser. In your search engine, search for the **Nimbus** Chrome extension. Click on the link to install it. You can see the Nimbus icon in the extension bar. Click on it and check the options available.

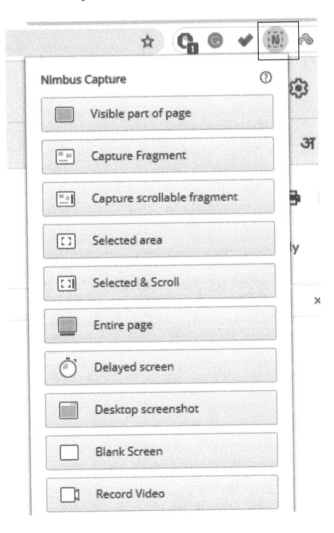

2. Now let us suppose you have to capture a long web page as a single image file, just open that web page and click on the **Entire page** option. The page will start scrolling itself, and you can see how much per cent of the page has been captured in the progress bar.

3. When finished, you will see the following screen. Click on the **Done** button.

4. You will be given the options to save the screenshot. You can save the page as an image file (png) or as a PDF

5. The Record option is of great use as it can record both a long web page and record a video playing in your browser.

   a. You can create a video of the long web page. Even if it has sound, that will also get recorded through the mic of your PC. After selecting the **Record Video** option, you need to scroll the page slowly. The nimbus extension will record the contents. When you are done, click on the **Stop** button to stop the video recording. Save the recording.

b. Suppose you want to capture a video playing in your browser. In that case, click **Start Record. Share your screen** dialog box appears.

c. Select the screen shown and click on the **Share** button. The screen will start getting recorded. When finished, stop the recording and save the video.

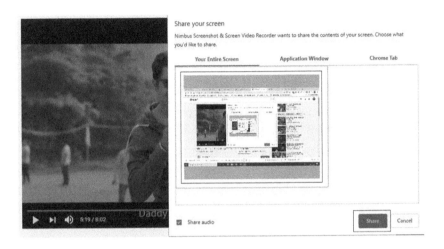

Note: Do also explore other options provided by the Nimbus option. Remember that it is the free version of the extension you are using, which is sufficient. Still, if you buy it, you will get much more functionality from it.

Producing a WhatsApp Chat as Digital Evidence

Consider a situation that you just had communication on WhatsApp with your tormentor. Now you have decided to file a complaint against him in the cyber cell. But before he deletes the messages sent to you, you must save that chat to be attached along with the filing of the complaint. The method is to export the complete chat by following the given steps:

1. Open the chat whose backup you want to create
2. Click on the three vertical dots on the rightmost corner
3. Click on the **More** option

4. Click on the **Export chat** option. You will be given options **Without media** or **Include Media** to export it. Click on the appropriate option.
5. Now you will be given choices on how to export it. You can do it by exporting it to another WhatsApp account or through an email and various other methods (we recommend doing it by using email).

The complete chat will be exported and can be produced as digital evidence now.

Conclusion

Readers have learnt what Digital Evidence is and its importance. They also learnt how to save and produce an email as a piece of digital evidence. They also got familiar with the Nimbus Chrome extension, capturing and recording a long web page as a single screenshot or video produced as digital evidence. Further collecting a complete WhatsApp chat as a piece of digital evidence has also been explained.

Multiple Choice Questions

1. Why is a piece of digital evidence important?
   a. To show it to your grandchildren
   b. To produce it with your complaint in the cyber cell
   c. To have it as a swag
   d. To experiment on it

2. What will you do when someone sends you an obscene message on a messaging app on your phone, and you want to produce that message as digital evidence?
   a. Take a picture of your phone
   b. Take a screenshot of the message
   c. Go to Cyber cell and submit your phone
   d. Start crying

3. The name of the extension which helps you save even a ten screen long web page as a single image is called:
   a. Nimboos
   b. Nimbus
   c. Minbus
   d. Niimbus

4. What advantage do you see in the Nimbus extension of having a recording facility?
   a. You can also record a video
   b. You can record youtube videos to watch later.
   c. You can use it for online teaching
   d. Ask who has authored this book

5. How many options do you see when you click on the Nimbus extension icon?
   a. 2
   b. 9
   c. 10
   d. Let me count

ANSWER KEY

1	2	3	4	5
b	b	b	a	c

LAB TIME

1. Open an email from your inbox and copy it as you have to produce it as digital evidence.

2. Open the website www.tccsweb.com. Save the complete home page as a single image and also as a video.

3. Open a video from YouTube and record it as you have to produce as digital evidence.

10

Debit/Credit Card Security

Scenario

On a Sunday, you are relaxing in the warmth of Sunlight, oblivious of the world. Suddenly you got a ping on your smartphone indicating that an SMS has arrived. You casually pick up the phone check. You suddenly jump up with a shock because the message reads $5000 (or currency of your country) have been deducted from your account. You are surprised as your ATM/Debit/Credit card is still in your pocket, and you have not been to any ATM in the last three days or did any shopping from your card, then what the hell it is?

Consider another example that you get a message that your credit card has been used to make an online purchase in Germany. The country which you even did not visit in your dreams. Are you terrified?

Overview

- Use of skimmers to extract details of your card
- Precautions to safeguard your card
- Some tricks which can be helpful in case you lost your card

DOI: 10.1201/9781003148678-11

Introduction to Skimmers

These types of frauds are topping the charts of cybercrime. It happens typically when your cards get cloned by someone, by getting details stored on a magnetic stripe and capturing the ATM PIN surreptitiously. Skimmers are used for this purpose.

To duplicate your card (clone it), the bad actor needs two things:

1. The details which are typically stored on the magnetic stripe (or chip) of the card
2. The ATM PIN

How Bad Actors Capture Your Card Details and ATM PIN

Many tricks can capture your card details at Point Of Sale Terminals (POS) or the ATM. Threat actors use the following method to get details when people use an ATM.

1. They capture the detail of your card with the help of ATM skimmers. They attach the skimmers over the real card slot of the ATM. When a clueless user enters the card in the card reader slot (now having a skimmer attached on top of it), all the details on the card's magnetic stripe get recorded.

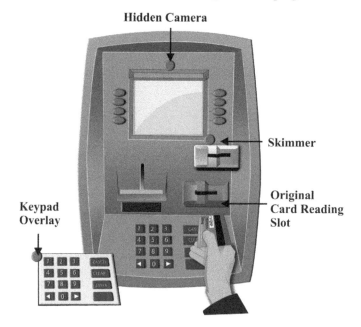

Hidden Camera

Skimmer

Original Card Reading Slot

Keypad Overlay

2. Now the bad actor needs to have your ATM PIN too. There are False PIN pad overlays that cover the actual ATM PIN pad. When a user enters the ATM PIN, the PIN gets recorded. Or there can be a camera inbuilt in the skimmer or brochure holder placed on the side of the ATM angled to capture the PIN you are entering.

3. After the details have been captured, the high-end skimmers can transfer the captured details by text message or wirelessly to the bad actor.

4. Blank cards and card cloners are available on many websites, and a duplicate of the original card gets created, and the transaction can happen anywhere in the country or abroad. This fraudulent transaction can occur either through an ATM or Online shopping.

Note: There are also ATM faceplates which are designed to cover the entire original ATM faceplate and can include anything from card readers to keypad overlays to hidden cameras.

What Is EMV?

EMV stands for Europay, MasterCard and Visa and refers to the increased security of payment made through card transactions by using a chip embedded in credit, debit and prepaid cards. EMV chip-based

cards are safer as they are very difficult (not impossible) to clone. But the irony is that most of the EMV chip cards also have a magnetic stripe at the back for backward compatibility with the ATMs/Swipe machines, which do not support EMV chip.

Protecting Yourself from Such Frauds

These types of frauds can be stopped to a more considerable extent by exercising some cautions, as mentioned below:

1. The chances of getting duped by a skimmer are higher on the weekend since most of the banks are closed on weekends, and it becomes harder for customers to report the suspicious ATMs to the bank. Criminals mostly install skimmers on Saturdays or Sundays and then remove them before the banks reopen on Monday.
2. Most skimmers are fixed on top of the existing card reader slot and obscure the flashing indicator. Be suspicious.
3. Gently slide the card slot to left and right, and also try pulling it. As these skimmers are temporarily fixed, they will come out.
4. Try to use the ATMs guarded by bank guards or, better, inside the banks.
5. While entering the PIN, always cover the keypad with one hand so that the PIN you are entering is not visible to anyone.

6. If you see suspect any glue around the PIN pad or see it is protruding a bit, do not use it.

7. Suppose if you have Near Field Communication (NFC) card, it is a wireless card. In that case, you do not have to swipe it at a POS terminal, but just hover it over the machine while making a payment. It is much safer and makes it very hard for bad actors to steal information from your card. Use cards that are NFC as well as have EMV chip.

8. In many countries, whenever online shopping is initiated, and after the Card Verification Value (CVV) is entered, an OTP (One Time Password) comes on the mobile phone number registered with the bank. That is not a mandatory practice in all countries. For example, in India, that OTP is compulsory, but whenever the transaction happens on a foreign payment gateway (maybe from inside India, like paying for buying Google Drive space), no OTP comes. The transaction gets completed after you enter the CVV, so do not depend much on OTPs. Take proper measures yourself.

9. A neat trick is to remove the CVV from the card, memorize it or better note it down somewhere else. That way, if your card gets stolen/lost, the person will not be able to use it in the ATM, as he/she does not have your ATM PIN. And, also not for online shopping as CVV is not there on the card. You are safe!

10. In case you lose your card, inform the bank immediately, preferably within 24 hours of it, and you can get back your lost money. Read conditions provided to you with the card. Those explain how, when, and where to report the loss of money due to the card's misuse.

11. Do prefer to do online shopping through credit cards. As with any transaction done through the debit card, the money is immediately deducted from the bank account. But in the case of credit cards, usually, transactions are processed in batches after a delay of hours/days. So there is a good chance to stop and reverse that transaction.

12. Never use and public computer or public Wi-Fi to do online shopping. It is very much possible that these public computers have some malware (maybe a keylogger) installed. That malware could be recording whatever you are typing and hence recording every detail of your card. And on public Wi-Fi, someone can capture the information in between which you are sending to the shopping website. That type of attack is called Man-in-The-Middle Attack (MITM). If you have to do online shopping using public Wi-Fi, always use a Virtual Private Network (VPN). That will encrypt your data and save your data from prying eyes.

13. Always do shopping from the websites starting from the HTTPS:// not HTTP://. The details transmitted from HTTPS:// websites are encrypted and can not be intercepted by criminals easily. HTTPS (Hypertext Transfer Protocol Secure) is an Internet communication protocol that provides a secure and private online experience when using a website. HTTPS has SSL (Secure Sockets Layer), which encrypts your information, so your connection is secured.

Note: One most important point to remember is, a phishing site, for example, can legitimately display its HTTPS address. Data sent through these sites are encrypted, but you cannot say that this site is not a phishing site or will not spread malware through it.

14. Avoid filling your card details in the survey forms, which claim that they will not use your card details without your permission.
15. Do not save your card details on any online shopping website even if you are prompted to do so. People usually do it because they do not need to re-enter details next time they shop from the same website. That makes the shopping process convenient, but suppose the company's server gets hacked. In that case, your financial data will also be compromised and misused or sold on the dark web.

Multiple Choice Questions

1. During online shopping, entering this is necessary to complete the shopping process:
   a. OTP
   b. CVV
   c. Both (a) and (b)
   d. None of the above

2. You can remove this from your card to protect against its misuse:
   a. Card number
   b. CVV
   c. Magnetic stripe
   d. Chip

3. While using your card on public Wi-Fi, always use this on your PC/smartphone:
   a. NPV
   b. VPN
   c. Proxy
   d. None of the above

4. Which one of these is correct?
   a. Always save your card detail on a shopping website
   b. You can use websites that claim that they will not use your card details
   c. Delete the CVV from your card
   d. None of the above

5. Which card is most secured?
   a. With magnetic stripe
   b. With EMV chip and magnetic stripe
   c. Only with EMV chip
   d. None of the above

6. It is a type of digital certificate that provides authentication for a website and enables an encrypted connection:
   a. SLS
   b. SSL
   c. HTTPS
   d. HTTP

ANSWER KEY

1	2	3	4	5	6
b	b	b	c	c	b

LAB TIME

1. Take your credit card/debit card in your hand and analyze it; which type of protection it has? Does it have an EMV chip or magnetic stripe, or both?
2. Next time you go to an ATM, survey the machine. Check carefully the slot where you insert the card and also the PIN Pad.
3. Find more about SSL.

11

WEBSITE HACKING AND SECURITY IMPLEMENTATION

Scenario

You have just got developed a website for your business. Unfortunately, it got hacked, and your client list been leaked out to your competitors. All this has resulted in bad press and financial loss for your company. So, now you are thinking about more stringent security measures for your website.

Hypothetically, if there is a cyberattack on the website, where there is a client data breach, it may result in lawsuits, hefty fines, and a ruined reputation of the company and the website.

Overview

- Concepts of website hacking and the significant threats waiting for your website when hackers found it vulnerable
- Website security and how one can protect it without being from a technical background

Introduction to Website Hacking

Websites have been on target lately and are highly under attack. Hackers are getting better at finding vulnerabilities in websites and exploiting them for their gain. As an Owner or an administrator, one should never be in this belief that their website is too small-scaled to be hacked. Nowadays, the hacking of websites has become extremely common. Therefore, having an appropriate security level for your website is very necessary.

DOI: 10.1201/9781003148678-12

Note: Website security is essential as a website is the online identity of an individual or a business. If a website is hacked and blacklisted, it usually loses most of its traffic. Not having a secure website is often as bad as not having a website in the least or maybe worse.

Website Vulnerability and Threats

Websites are highly vulnerable to the most common vulnerabilities, which should always be taken care of. These vulnerabilities are such that they might seem small to you, but they might leak information worth a lot. The most common types of web vulnerabilities are listed below:

SQL Injection

It is commonly known as SQLi, typically an injection attack that is supposed to execute any malicious SQL code on a database server. The attacker can delete, execute, extract hidden and confidential information or modify these critical databases (which stores all the confidential entries).

XSS

XSS stands for Cross-Site Scripting, which technically means that the attacker injects malicious client-side script on the website. The attacker can control the victim's web browser or an account on the vulnerable web application.

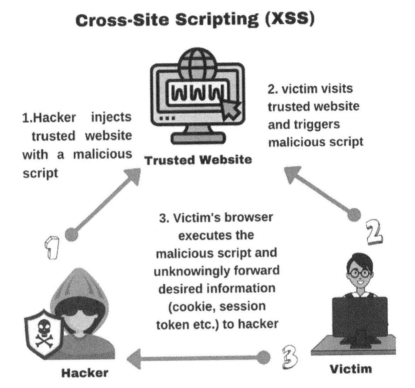

DoS and DDoS

It stands for denial-of-service (DoS) attacks where the attacker intends to make the website unavailable to the users by flooding the target website's traffic.

Note: A distributed denial-of-service (DDoS) attack is that attack in which multiple compromised computer systems attack a target (such as a server, website or other network resources). That causes a denial of service for users of the targeted resource.

Brute Force Attack

Brute Force Attack is a technique when hackers employ specific automated tools to provide them with thousands of various combinations of words, numbers and special characters to break the admin panel's login details.

Dictionary Attack

Dictionary Attack is similar to the Brute Force Attack. In this attack, the hacker, instead of combinations, tries dictionary words to guess your password or creates a word-list of common and stolen credentials to break the admin panel's login details. It work faster than the Brute Force attack

Website Security

Website security is a critical topic that a website owner should pay attention to. Leaving the website vulnerable might lead to bringing down the website's reputation, expenses of loss in business and many more adverse effects.

To provide necessary security to a website, it is not essential to be tech-savvy or have a computer background. The things one can do to secure a website from potential threats:

Purchasing a Hosting Service

While you are buying a website domain name and hosting service, buy it from a reliable and secure web hostings provider like Godaddy.com or bluehost.com or such others. They regularly update their servers with the latest software and scripts; they scan their servers regularly for known malware with the right antivirus solutions. They constantly monitor all files present on their servers.

Take Care of the Hosting Plan You Choose

Suppose you are a big organization, and your name and reputation matter a lot. In that case, logically, you should be able and willing to spend a respectable amount on securing your website. Purchase a dedicated IP Address (Public IP address) and a dedicated hosting plan for your website. It is so that no other site is sharing your IP address, as in the case of regular hosting in which they provide a *shared IP address* in a *shared hosting* plan. Remember that a website launched on a shared IP Address is not as secure as a website launched on a dedicated IP Address. A dedicated IP costs a little more, but the website becomes completely safe. If you expect lots of website traffic and sensitive data on the website, consider buying a dedicated hosting plan too. Usually, when you purchase a website, the hosting provider offers an inexpensive domain name and hosting plan, which you should avoid if your website contains sensitive data. Research properly before buying a hosting plan, as there are many such plans are available (including VPS hosting), and you can pick the one which suits you and secure your website too.

SSL Certificates

They protect the information that travels through your website. For example, information filled in forms and credit/debit card numbers, as it is transferred from a website to another server to store it. It is a very basic web-security measure, and one must get it. These days, most popular browsers and search engines are labeling sites without SSL as "insecure," which could make visitors suspicious of your site. One should remember that an SSL encrypts and protects data in transit from prying eyes, so take further steps to secure the website.

Software Updates

Websites hosted on a content management (CMS) system are always at the risk of compromise. Thanks to vulnerabilities and security issues often found in third-party plugins and applications. These are often prevented by installing updates to plugins and core software promptly, as these updates often contain security patches. Since WordPress is the most used CMS to develop websites, here is the list of plugins to implement to make it secure. Remember to type the URL exactly as it is, taking care of upper-case and lower-case letters.

Bullet Proof Security - Download from http://bit.ly/3aG8mbG
Word fence - Download from http://bit.ly/2ZCL93J
iThemes Security - Download from http://bit.ly/3aG8BDC
All In One WP Security & Firewall - Download from http://bit.ly/2ZDQHLC
Sucuri - Download from http://bit.ly/3qOmx4g
Fail2ban - Download from http://bit.ly/3stmcV5

Note: Examples of the most widely used open-source CMS platforms include: WordPress, Joomla, Drupal, Magento and Shopify.

Website Scanning

After you have successfully developed a website, scan it with web vulnerabilities detection scanners. These scanners try to scan your website for all well-known vulnerabilities or test all known exploits by trying to compromising your site. Here are some popular website scanners:

Acunetix (Paid): It is a popular web vulnerability scanner, and we also recommend you to use this scanner. 70% of the websites and networks can be hacked into, according to the Acunetix website's information. You can get a demo of Acunetix software from www.acunetix.com. A better option is to purchase this scanning software if you are planning to do a job as a Penetration Tester.

Netsparker (Paid): It is another web vulnerability scanner for which you can arrange a demo from www.netsparker.com. The trial of this scanner is free for a few days. You will find vulnerabilities like SQL Injection and Cross-site Scripting (XSS) and other security flaws on all websites and web applications with this scanner.

Web-Application Firewall

It is meant to stop automated attacks that commonly target small or lesser-known websites. These attacks are performed by malicious agents that automatically search for vulnerabilities in the websites and exploit them or cause DDoS attacks that slow or crash your website.

Stop Using Public Computers/Wi-Fi to Access the Website Dashboard

If you manage the website yourself, you need to access the dashboard of your hosting company and the admin area (Login Page) frequently. Do not do this by using public computers/Wi-Fi. By doing so, you are essentially putting yourself in a position where you are prey for hackers. Don't believe any cafe owner, even if he or she looks legitimate, because the hacker could have installed hacking software as a key logger on public computers at cafes.

Login Attempts to Be Limited

Have you ever visited a bank website? There if you provide the wrong username and incorrect password on your login page a few times, you will be locked out of your account. Your login attempts are limited to 3 or 5, and then you will be blocked access for a temporary period or until you answer all your security questions and such. Like the functioning of a bank website, you can also limit login attempts on your website's admin page. If you have got your website developed by other developers, don't forget to implement this feature on your website's login page. Developers can code this feature on the login page to limit login attempts to secure the site from attacks like Brute Force Attack or Dictionary Attack.

For developers who have developed their websites using WordPress, Plugins are available in the WordPress plugins directory. You can easily install WordPress plugins to limit login attempts on the login page.

Making a Backup of Your Website

You should make a backup of your website files and database. Many automated tools can make a backup of your website and mail you the backup files. The latest backup is essential when you have to restore the site. Many service providers provide automatic daily backup at some extra cost. You should also know how to take backup and restore the backup website instead of always being dependent on the web developer.

Tracking Website Logs Regularly

If you can check logs of visitors on your site from cPanel, then once a week, spare some time to check on visitors' IP addresses to your website regularly. If you track any abnormal traffic like numbers of visits from different countries, from where you do not expect any traffic, then be vigilant. Try to implement all security measures, as there could be someone trying to hack your website.

Note: cPanel is an online Linux-based graphical interface (GUI). It is used as a control panel to simplify and monitor website and server management.

Purchasing Protection, Monitoring and Repair Service

As additional security measures, you can get website protection services from a company like CloudFare. They are well known for protecting & securing any website online. You can visit them at https://www.cloudflare.com. Cloudflare even protects the site from DDoS (Distributed Denial of Service) attacks on a website.

Let's Do It! – Checking Which Hosting Plan Your Hosting Provider Has Given to You

Also, check whether your website is on a shared IP address or a dedicated IP address.

1. Browse www.yougetsignal.com/tools/web-sites-on-web-server/
2. Enter the domain of the website (without https://www) and click the **Check** option.
   a. You will get a list of all domain names launched on the same web server, and many even share the same IP address.
   b. Suppose you get several unknown websites launched on the same web server and share the same IP as your website. In that case, you must contact the hosting company to ask them to provide a dedicated IP address.

The "Reverse IP Domain Check" link takes a domain name or IP address and searches for other sites hosted on the same web server.

Reverse IP Domin Check

Remote Address: | Chandigarhciticenter.com | | Check |

Found 40 domains hoeted on the same web server as chandigarhciticenter.com (182.50.151.35)

2020kk.com
exiger.co.in
activete-setup.com
www.ineedtrip.com
www.blulkssms.com
....
....
....
....
....
....

377606.com
ahrc.in
w3schools.com
www.bulkssms.com
www.tri-phil.com
....
....
....
....
....
....

About

A reverse IP domain check takes a domain name or IP address pointing to a web server and searches for other sites known to be hosted on that same web server. Data is gathered from search engine results, which are not guaranteed to be complete. IP-Address.org provides interesting visual reverse IP lookup tool. Knowing the other web sites hosted on a web server is important from both an SEO and web filtering perspective, particularly for those on shared web hosting plans.

Note: The typical standard plan we get is shared IP in a shared hosting plan. As per the above screenshot, you note down the IP address and do a reverse domain check for other domain names shown. You will find many are sharing the same IP address too. If your website has sensitive data, at least buy a Dedicated IP in the shared hosting plan. The best option is still buying a dedicated IP in a dedicated hosting plan.

Conclusion

Hence, the readers are now aware of website security's importance and the repercussions of having a website without proper security measures. Readers who are not tech-savvy can now secure their websites, so they don't need prior knowledge and experience in cybersecurity. They can also give directions to their web developer to implement these steps.

Multiple Choice Questions

1. The following is a reputed Website hosting provider:
   a. Gomommy, com
   b. Godaddy.com
   c. Gofriend.com
   d. None of the above

2. The following is used to scan your mentioned website for vulnerability thoroughly:
   a. Netparker
   b. Nertsparker
   c. Starparker
   d. Carparker

3. WordPress Website admin panel can be secured by (Tick any two):
   a. Limiting the login attempts
   b. Removing limit to login attempts
   c. You can get website protection services from a company like Cloudflare.
   d. None of the above

4. Which is the most secured hosting plan?
   a. Shared IP in shared hosting
   b. Dedicated IP in shared hosting
   c. Dedicated IP in Dedicated hosting
   d. None of the above

5. Which one of these is not the website vulnerability scanner?
   a. Acunetix
   b. OpenVAS
   c. Nessus
   d. Impact Bore

ANSWER KEY

1	2	3	4	5
b	b	a,c	c	d

LAB TIME

1. Find out which hosting plan you have for your website. If you do not have a website, check it for some unknown or a friend's website. Talk to the customer care of the website hosting company to find out the cost of changing to a dedicated IP (if it is not a dedicated IP already).
2. Get a demo from Acunetix for your website.

12

PROTECTION FROM EMAIL SPOOFING

Scenario

For the pandemic 2021, you have got an email from the World Health Organization (WHO) that vaccine of Covid-19 has arrived in your Country. The emails say to click on the link enclosed to check further details on registering for the vaccination procedure. You got excited, and without verifying the details of the sent email, you clicked on the link. But you did not find anything valuable on the web page where that link directed to you. So, you closed the link. And after a few days, you realized that webcam of your laptop had been hacked. You came to know about it because somebody sent you a video on your messaging app that was recorded through the laptop's webcam placed in your bedroom.

That is a terrifying thing that can happen to anyone. The person did not realize that although the email was showing the source as WHO, but was from some illegitimate source.

Objectives

- Methods to check a spoofed email
- Analyzing the email header to get the source

Introduction to Email Spoofing

Email spoofing is the forgery of an email sender address so that the message appears to have come from someone other than the actual source. For example, the sender's name could show AMAZON, but the mail has been spoofed and sent by some bad actor. It is not difficult to send a fake email to someone by spoofing someone's email ID. That has made it essential to identify the source of the email.

DOI: 10.1201/9781003148678-13

Method I

Hovering the Pointer over the Sender's Name

In the usual way, it does not take much expertise to know the actual sender. Just hover the mouse pointer over the sender's name (Here, WHO), and you can see the source domain name (here, Bank of Baroda). Below is the image; you can see how hovering the pointer over sender's name is unmasking the original domain name.

Method II

Analyzing the Header of the Email

You must know that each email received has a header. Email headers contain crucial information. The information can include the sender and receiver's name, the path (servers and other devices) through which the message has travelled, and many different types of information are stored there.

Some websites can analyze the header and get the source IP. From that source IP, it becomes easy to get further geolocation details to confirm the email's originating place. Let us see how to do it. Since Gmail is the most popular email provider, we will be analyzing the header of an email received in a Gmail account.

1. Open the email from your inbox (remember, just open, do not click on any link or download any attachment).
2. Click on three dots and click on select the **Show Original** option.

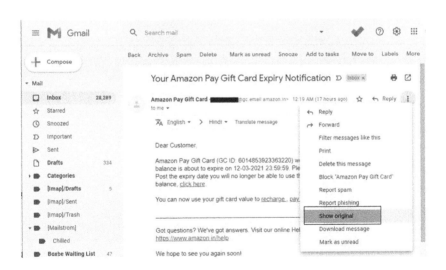

3. Start selecting the header from the beginning until the body text (as shown in the image), Right-click and select the **Copy** option.

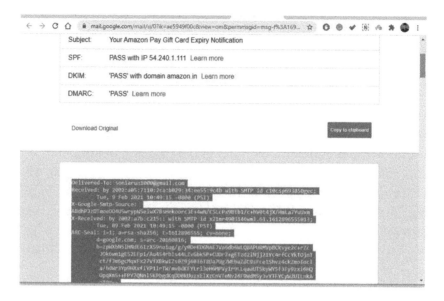

4. In a new tab of your web browser:
   a. Open the website www.whatismyip.com. Click on the **Email Header Analyzer** button.
   b. In the box, paste the copied matter and click on the Analyze button. The result will show you the IP address of the source and details of the ISP.

5. You will see the required details

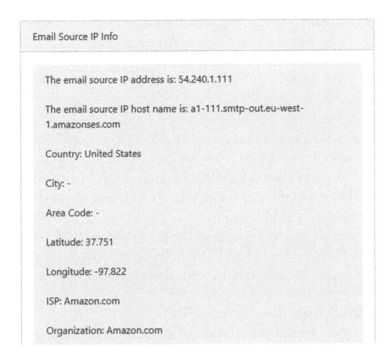

Email Source IP Info

The email source IP address is: 54.240.1.111

The email source IP host name is: a1-111.smtp-out.eu-west-1.amazonses.com

Country: United States

City: -

Area Code: -

Latitude: 37.751

Longitude: -97.822

ISP: Amazon.com

Organization: Amazon.com

6. We will also confirm the details further from another website. Open www.whatismyipaddress.com. Click on the **IP LOOKUP** button. Enter the IP address and click on the **Get IP Details** button. You will see the geolocation details for that IP address.

Method III

Check for SPF, DKIM and DMARK

These seem to be alien terms but are becoming industry standard to check and constrain for email spoofing.

It is also possible to spoof the domain name. Then it becomes challenging to identify a spoofed email. Attackers can spoof a sender's email address because the Simple Mail Transfer Protocol (SMTP) doesn't provide email ID authentication. Also, poorly configured email servers are without any email security protection against cybercriminals.

Organizations can implement email address authentication mechanisms that work together to protect against email spoofing. These are **Sender Policy Framework (SPF), Domain Keys Identified Mail (DKIM), Domain-based Message Authentication, Reporting and Conformance (DMARC)**.

This method to check the spoofed email is very simple. You need to check for SPF, DKIM and DMARK fields while analyzing an email's header. The following are what these terms mean:

SPF: Sender Policy Framework

DKIM: Domain Keys Identified Mail

DMARC: Domain-based Message Authentication, Reporting & Conformance.

- SPF helps servers verify that messages are coming from a genuine source. It means messages appearing to come from a particular domain are sent from servers that the domain owner approves.
- DKIM adds a digital signature to every message. It lets receiving servers verify that the message is not fake and was not changed during transit.
- DMARC enforces SPF and DKIM authentication. It lets admins get reports about message authentication and delivery.

Let's Do It! – Checking for SPF, DKIM and DMARK

Follow the given steps:

1. Open the email from your inbox (remember, just open, do not click on any link or download any attachment from it.
2. Click on three dots and click on select the **Show Original** option
3. Now look for all three parameters. If all are PASS, it means the email is safe and not spoofed.

Original Message

Message ID	<125316969.39140696.1626002391629@mbkafka7848>
Created at:	Sun, Jul 11, 2021 at 4:49 PM (Delivered after 2 seconds)
From:	Magic█████ <support@r███bricks.com>
To:	soniarun1000@gmail.com
Subject:	You're missing out on Leads! Upgrade your Ad pack now to connect
SPF:	PASS with IP 103.18.143.56 Learn more
DKIM:	'PASS' with domain magicbricks.com Learn more
DMARC:	'PASS' Learn more

So while opening an email, use all three methods to ensure that the email is from the legitimate source and not spoofed.

Note: If you own a website and are using that, send messages to your customers. Make sure that you implement these three on your Domain, too, so nobody can misuse your domain name to send unauthenticated and spoofed emails from your domain name. You can take the help of your website developer to implement these for your domain name. It is the best way to stop spoofing your domain name.

Conclusion

In this chapter, the reader will know what email spoofing, and its implications. Also, they learnt to check the email received is fake or genuine by learning to analyze email headers. Do not forget to scan the attachment with a trusted antivirus before you double-click to open it.

Multiple Choice Questions

1. To analyze a header from a received email, which website and button will you use?
   a. Whatismyip.com and Email Header Analyzer button
   b. Whatismyipaddress.com and E-mail Header Analyzer button
   c. What is your IP and Email Header Analyzer button
   d. None of the above

2. Which link in www.whatismyipaddress.com is used to check details of some IP address?
   a. Lookup IP
   b. IP Lookup
   c. IP for Lookup
   d. IP Analyzer

3. Which one of the following is used to check the integrity of the email message?
   a. SPF
   b. DKIM
   c. DMARC

4. Which one of the following is used to check the authorized sender?
   a. SPF
   b. DKIM
   c. DMARC

5. Do you think that implement SPF, DKIM and DMARC will result emails from your Domain name to go in the inbox of a receiver that in a SPAM folder?
   a. Yes
   b. No
   c. Sometimes
   d. Why are you asking?

ANSWER KEY

1	2	3	4	5
a	b	b	a	a

LAB TIME

1. Open an email from the inbox and use all three methods to check whether it is genuine or a spoofed email.
2. Find some other websites (other than whaismyip.com) which can analyze the header of your email.
3. Analyze an email header and find out the source IP and other details related to it.

13

BACKUP AND ENCRYPTION

Scenario

Let's look at a situation where you have been working from home for an enterprise and have sensitive data in your system. Suddenly one morning, when you boot up your system, you get a message that your data (hard drive) has been encrypted (made non-readable). The files will be decrypted after paying a certain amount by a deadline to the attacker. Let's say you already have the latest backup of your device's data stored in a secured drive. You can ignore the intruder's warning, format your PC, and reload data from the backup you had. All is good!

Let us go further. You have the latest backup, but now the intruder is blackmailing you that your data is in control of him and will be leaked to your competitors if you do not pay a certain amount. It is a scary situation because even your backup is of no use now. Are you thinking of a solution?

Here the encryption comes into the scene. Suppose you have already encrypted your sensitive data, and the intruder takes control of your computer. In that case, it will be useless for him/her as the data is in an encrypted form, and it is only you who can decrypt the data.

Objectives

- Ransomware's basic working and how one can lose their data to a cybercriminal
- The concept of backup & encryption of data as proactive protection from ransomware attacks
- Introducing BitLocker and VeraCrypt
- Practically using BitLocker to encrypt a drive

Introduction to Ransomware

Ransomware is a type of malware that encrypts the files on the affected system, making them inaccessible, and demands a payment

DOI: 10.1201/9781003148678-14

to restore access. The ransom demand usually comes with a deadline. If the person does not pay the ransom, the data is not decrypted or made public for competitors to see.

Ransomware attacks have become very common and pervasive in small and large organizations that are hugely affecting businesses. Today's cybercriminals have become highly creative and use various ways to influence the system. They use social engineering to convince targets to click on some malicious link, resulting in ransomware affecting the data.

Major government agencies like the FBI have been advising Internet users from paying any ransom to these criminals, which may encourage them to infiltrate more systems in the future. Also, there is a very bleak chance that you will get back your data even after paying the ransom.

There are ways where one can still protect their data against ransomware attacks by making use of data encryption software and performing a timely backup of data.

Working of Ransomware Attacks

Cybercriminals generally use phishing techniques to deliver the ransomware into the devices of victims. The victims once download the files in their system; many things can be done using the malware, including encrypting of data.

The encryption intensity (mathematical scrambling of input data) depends on the sophistication of the algorithm. The user should be aware that it is nearly impossible to decrypt this data without the attacker's key. Users have then displayed a ransom message on the screen asking for payment in crypto currency so that their identity remains unknown.

Cybercriminals generally rely on the user's fear of losing the data, which may compel them to pay the hefty ransom under a quickly running timer. Backup of your entire data is the most recommended form of defense to prevent the ransomware infection from occurring. Moreover, always have sensitive files in an encrypted format. Even if the attacker somehow can intrude into your system, the sensitive data remains unreadable to him.

WannaCry, CryptoLocker, TeslaCrypt, SimpleLocker, NotPetya, Cerber etc., have been some of the worst ransomware the world has seen in the last five years.

Backup and Its Importance

Backup is the process of creating a copy of the data on your system that you use for recovery in case your original data is lost or corrupted because of any reason. If a user's system is infected with ransomware, one can escape it without paying the ransom. It is only possible when the user is already prepared with a backup of the entire drive or essential files. Taking backups is generally necessary for every individual system as we never know when one can get affected by the ransomware. One can end up losing all the crucial data in a fraction of seconds.

However, no one can ensure that the user's backup is also secure from the attackers. After creating multiple copies, it is also recommended that those are stored in different locations. The users should also use external storage devices and upload the backup on a cloud platform online. By doing this, the user can let go of the ransom demand without losing any data.

Note: The 3-2-1 backup rule is a simpler term for a common approach to keeping your data safe in almost any failure circumstance The rule is: keep at least three (3) copies of the data, and store two (2) backup copies on different storage media, with one (1) of them located off-site or on the cloud.

Importance of Data Encryption

Data encryption can be defined as translating the original data into another form, which could be a code or something that anyone cannot understand and can only be accessed using a decryption key or a password as preferred by a user. It is one of the most effective forms of data protection. Encryption intends to provide confidentiality of the data stored in the system or the network.

Keeping the above thought in mind, users should consider data encryption as a data protection method that will effectively act against a ransomware attack favoring the user. Encryption of data will protect the data in any condition when the encryption key is secured and turns out to be useless for the attacker.

Backing up the data and encrypting it may look like a complicated and time-consuming process. Still, it is an effective solution against ransomware attacks.

Encrypting Data Using BitLocker

BitLocker is the encryption technology provided by Windows. It protects your data from unauthorized access by encrypting your drive. Then to access it, one requires one or more factors of authentication before it will unlock it.

Note: BitLocker is available to anyone who has a machine running Windows Vista or 7 Ultimate, Windows Vista or 7 Enterprise, Windows 8.1 Pro, Windows 8.1 Enterprise, or Windows 10 Pro. Standard versions of Windows does not include the BitLocker feature.

Let's Do It! – Encrypting a Drive Using the BitLocker

1. Search BitLocker in the search box in Windows 10. Click on the **Manage BitLocker** link.
2. The drives available with BitLocker options will get displayed. Click on the **Turn On BitLocker** option. The BitLocker will start for that drive and will ask for the password. Enter the password and click on the **Next** button.

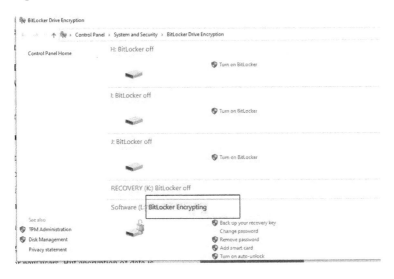

3. After entering the password, the drive will get encrypted and accessed by entering the password only.

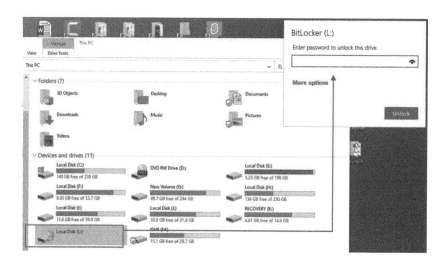

Encrypting Data Using VeraCrypt

VeraCrypt is a free open source software that you can easily download for Windows, Linux or Mac systems. It can create a virtual encrypted disk within a file or encrypt a partition or the entire storage device with pre-boot authentication. If your Windows version does not have BitLocker, use the VeraCrypt encrypting software. Remember that encryption with VeraCrypt is a little tricky. So it is advisable to read some tutorial related to it before using the VeraCrypt software.

Using Anti Ransomware Feature of an Antivirus

Operating BitLocker and VeraCrypt can be a tedious process for new users. But encryption of data is a must if you have to protect your sensitive data. These days most Antivirus software comes with ransomware protection. The software will ask which folder(s)/drive you want to protect from ransomware. Just select the folder, and that folder will become encrypted and protected from ransomware protected. **Trend Micro Antivirus+** is such an Antivirus/malware software through which I encrypted one of my folder on the Desktop and my USB Drive.

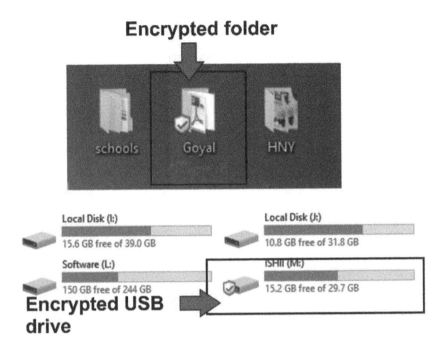

Conclusion

In this chapter, the readers have been acquainted with ransomware's potential harm. They also learned how to protect themselves from losing sensitive data to cybercriminals and prevent themselves from paying any ransom by using backups and encrypting their data.

Multiple Choice Questions

1. The function of the ransomware is:
   a. Decrypt the data
   b. Encrypt the data
   c. Make it invisible
   d. None of the above

2. This is an encryption software:
   a. Foldercrypt
   b. LockerBit
   c. VeraCrypt
   d. None of the above

3. Which of these is a strong encrypted form of "I am a good boy"?
   a. I a good boy am
   b. 9cx24#%4eECb
   c. 128 a good boy
   d. Boy good a am I

4. A good password consists of:
   a. Only text
   b. Only numbers and text
   c. Combination of lowercase, uppercase, numbers and symbols
   d. None of the above

5. BitLocker is available in all variants of Windows edition:
   a. Yes
   b. No
   c. None of the above
   d. I do not care

ANSWER KEY

1	2	3	4	5
b	c	b	c	b

LAB TIME

1. Find out, do you have BitLocker in your Windows OS? If you have, encrypt a drive with it.
2. Create a folder with the name "Mydata" on your disk, and encrypt it.
3. Encrypt the data in your USB drive.
4. Find more software from the Web which can encrypt your folders.

14

MUST-HAVE APPS FOR WOMEN AND ELDERLY

Scenario

These times are problematic, especially for women. We are always worried about our female family members. Even when our daughters and sisters go for tuitions, evil thoughts keep nudging us. Have they reached the coaching center? Moreover, if they get late by 15 minutes from the scheduled time, our mind becomes a storehouse of worries. The same is the case with elderly parents. We are always worried even when they go for a walk in the park. Thoughts like, what if a health emergency happens with them, always remain with us.

Overview

- The necessity of using apps for Women and elderly
- Recommendation and features of some selected Apps

Introduction to Emergency Apps

We can pass on this burden of thoughts on technology. Some apps can be of immense help in case of emergencies. Still, most of them are not quality apps, and it is very time-consuming to find good quality and high-performance apps. Here, we have researched and recommended some useful apps for your close ones about whom you are constantly worried.

We have researched a lot to find the most appropriate and high-quality apps which will be helpful. You can download these apps and follow the app instructions to test those. One or two such apps are sufficient on your smartphone. You can try all apps and select the most convenient for you to use. These apps can prove to be lifesavers

DOI: 10.1201/9781003148678-15

in emergencies like sexual harassment, stalking or medical emergencies. By just pressing a button, you can notify your selected contacts within your location that some crisis has come up and you need help.

How Do These Emergency Apps Work?

Most of the apps work like this:

1. You create an emergency contact list. When in trouble, tap the SOS button (some apps work even when you scream and the phone is in your bag or pocket). The App will send an SMS alert with the location detail to your emergency contact phone numbers. The Chilla App is a good example of that, which takes action even on screaming.

2. Many apps allow you to create a group of contacts that you want to track. Those contacts' live location will always be shared to you by apps, and you can track them easily and continuously. Many apps enable you to get all the real-time information about your close ones' movement, location, battery percentage, signal strength, and travelling speed. Also, apps like CitizenCop gives you options to quickly find the nearest hospitals, police stations, restaurants, Petrol pumps etc. and provide you with a call option.

3. You can create a safety zone like a market, school, and college for your close one. When that person leaves that circle, you will get notification, and when he again enters the safety zone, you will get notified.

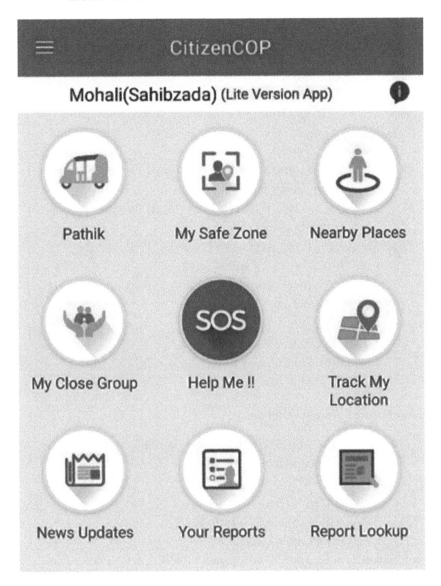

Always use Apps that have no advertisements. Of course, when there is an emergency to click the SOS Panic button, you do not want to see the ad for innerwear for 7 seconds. Most of the apps reviewed are free without advertisements. Some good ones are paid too. It is better to buy a paid one without advertisement than free with ads.

Recommended Apps for Android Phones

1. Smart24x7 Personal Safety App – by Smart24x7 – For Android and iOs
   Link: http://bit.ly/3qJ1orV
2. Disha SOS – by Andhra Pradesh police – For Android and iOs
   Link: http://bit.ly/3kbsqpr
3. My Safetipin: Complete Safety App – by Safepin
   Link: http://bit.ly/3ug7VNb
4. TrackiGPS-Track Cars, Kids, Pets, Assets & More – Tracki
   Link: http://bit.ly/3ug7VNb
5. CitizenCop – By Quacito/INFOCRATS
   Link: http://bit.ly/3aGs9rn
6. Chilla – Women safety app with scream detection – By Kishlay Raj Products
   Link: http://bit.ly/3pHvqLB
7. Safe Family Circle – RT Tijerina
   Link: http://bit.ly/3khwEvN

Recommended Apps for iPhones

1. My Safetipin – By Active learning Solutions
   Link: http://apple.co/3sdxbBI
2. Tracki GPS – Tracki inc
   http://apple.co/3bq8pHK
3. CitizenCOP – Quacito/INFOCRATS
   Link: http://apple.co/3aIp5v7
4. Safemily – Family GPS Locator – INVODEV
   http://apple.co/3qDjdZs

Note: CitizenCOP is a Not for Profit foundation that has impacted over 5 million lives throughout India's multiple cities by bridging the gap between the citizens and the police through an app. It acts as a uniform platform while promoting safety, empowerment and convenience. It uses a bundle of compelling features like reporting lost articles/incidents, SOS and many more available for global use effortlessly.

Some great fetaures of CitizenCop app

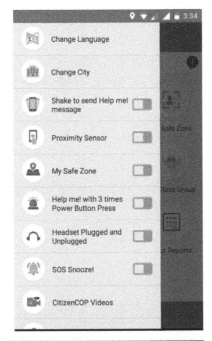

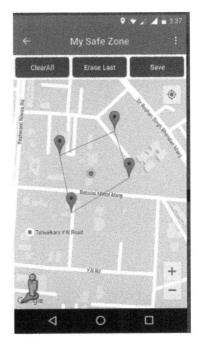

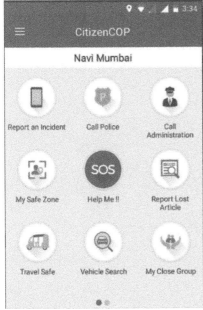

Conclusion

This chapter explains how to leverage existing apps to safeguard ourselves (mostly ladies, children and the elderly). Have at least one App that can notify your selected contacts in case of emergency. If you always remain worried about your loved ones' location and well-being, install an app that can create a group and continuously update you about their live location.

Multiple Choice Questions

1. This one is the valid name of the App mentioned in this chapter:
   a. Tracky GPS
   b. Trackie GPS
   c. Tricky GPS
   d. Tyricky GPS

2. No app can give you live location of your close ones who are always travelling:
   a. True
   b. False
   c. I do not know
   d. I do not want to track anyone

3. This App gives you options to quickly find nearest hospitals, police stations, restaurants, petrol pumps, etc., and also call the same immediately irrespective of where you are:
   a. CitiCop
   b. CitizenCop
   c. Tricky
   d. Chilla

4. This App can activate the SOS button even on your scream:
   a. CitizenCop
   b. Tricki GPS
   c. Chilla
   d. None of the above

5. These safety apps are great ways to socialize and share cooking recipes:
   a. Yes
   b. No
   c. Maybe
   d. I do not know

ANSWER KEY

1	2	3	4	5
b	b	b	c	b

LAB TIME

1. Test all the apps one by one, check their functionality and ease of use. Select and install one on your smartphone.
2. Test the installed App with your family members.
3. Install an app on your mobile phone, create a group of all your close ones and use that App to track people in the group.

15

PENETRATION TESTING USING A SMARTPHONE

Scenario

Suddenly you realize that the speed of your Wi-Fi connection has dropped down. You test it through https://www.speedtest.net/. Oh Yes! Instead of 100 MBPS, it is showing 26 MBPS. You call up the customer care cell of your ISP and explain your problem. The customer care representative assures you that you are getting 100 MBS from the backend and advises you to check at your end. You are confused. Where is the glitch? Has your Wi-Fi been hacked, and more people are using it in an unauthorized manner? Because more devices are connected to the Wi-Fi, the bandwidth is being shared, affecting speed.

You might often be worried about the security of your digital systems and the network connecting them. You are worried continuously about whether an attacker would breach your privacy and might take advantage of any vulnerability available in your devices and network.

Suppose you have critical information that you cannot afford to lose at any cost or may impact your business hugely. In that case, you need to secure your digital network. So, let's focus on what you can do to find out the potential threats in your systems and network and how you can overcome them. Although it is an elaborate testing procedure, we can use some useful Smartphone apps that can test the security of the network for our home network.

Objectives

After studying this chapter, you should be able to:

- Have a better understanding of penetration testing, why it needs to be performed, and its different types
- Understand the various phases of penetration testing and the advantages of penetration testing

- Step-by-step perform penetration testing of your home network/website using apps in Smartphones

Introduction to Penetration Testing

Penetration testing is usually referred to as pen-testing. It is a method of assessing systems and networks' security by performing simulated attacks to find the vulnerabilities that an attacker could exploit. Performing pen-testing usually bring out the threats in your security model and helps you patch them before they can be exploited.

Pen-testing will identify the vulnerabilities and also define the criticality of the attack with a detailed report. It should be only performed on the permission of the required authority given in writing to the pen-tester. Otherwise, it might result in cybercrime, although it was performed with the right intentions. All companies which deal with electronic data should get pen-testing occasionally performed to confirm that their IT infrastructure is safe.

Why Is Penetration Testing Performed?

- To test and approve the serenity measures in systems and networks
- To identify the threats if present in systems or networks
- To take necessary measures to prevent any attack due to the exploitation of vulnerabilities

Types of Penetration Testing

Types of penetration testing depend on the information you have as a pen-tester about the systems and networks. The penetration testing can be of the following types:

White-Box Testing

This type of testing is performed when detailed information about the systems and network is given to the pen-tester. It is usually referred to as complete-knowledge testing as the pen-tester knows the resources.

Black-Box Testing

This type of testing is usually referred as zero-knowledge testing as it is performed without any prior information of the system and network to the pen-tester. The tester can apply any method of choice to perform pen-testing to find out the vulnerabilities. This process might consume a lot of time and may turn expensive.

Gray-Box Testing

This type is a combination of white and black box testing and is also referred to a partial knowledge testing. We can define it as a simulated attack performed by a pen-tester posing as an attacker with limited privileges.

Phases of Penetration Testing

Pen-testing is divided into different phases.

1. *Planning*
    It includes defining the scope and the goal of the pen-test to be performed.
2. *Reconnaissance*
    It usually involves gathering all the available information on the target to perform the pen-test.
3. *Threat Modeling*
    This step usually involves identifying threats.
4. *Vulnerability Assessment*
    After the identification of threats, vulnerability is assessed based on their criticalities.
5. *Exploitation*
    It involves exploiting the vulnerabilities obtained in the previous steps.
6. *Post Exploitation*
    This step involves the ideas and methods to fix the exploited vulnerability.

7. *Reporting*

This step involves generating a report after penetration testing is complete.

Limited Penetration Testing Using Smartphone

In this tech-savvy world, smartphones are much in demand. You can use your android and iOS devices to perform limited pen-testing at your convenience so that you don't need to carry a bulky system. A pen-tester can use a specific set of tools to penetrate a network or computer system with your Smartphone's help. Of course, not detailed pen testing can be carried out, but still, you can secure your home network up to a more considerable extent.

Let's do it! – Using the Network Scanner App

Network Scanner (by zoltan pallagi) is a tool that can be downloaded in Android devices for Network testing. It gives you a list of devices connected to a network and much more information.

1. Download the Network Scanner app from here from Google play store: (https://play.google.com/store/apps/details?id=com.pzolee.networkscanner)
   (short link: http://bit.ly/network-scanner)
   Once you download it, click on the icon to open it.
2. Click on the **Start button**, and you will be able to see all the devices connected to your network, with their name and IP

address and the MAC address. Now you can analyze that if you have four devices currently connected to Wi-Fi, why it is showing more devices. It means some unauthorized persons are having access to your Wi-Fi. Remember that the IP address is the unique address allocated to any device connected to a network and can change.

MAC address is the unique physical address assigned to a device by the manufacturer and is unchangeable. It is also unique but does not get forwarded with messages or website visits, like an IP address. When you notice that more than the required devices are connected to your Wi-Fi, your next step should be changing your Wi-Fi password and checking that you have the most robust encryption (WPA2 or WPA3) enabled.

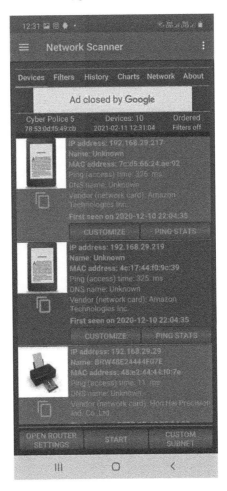

3. Click on the **History tab.** You can see on which the previous date you connected to which Wi-Fi network and how many devices were there on that Wi-Fi network (**Load All option is available in paid version only**).

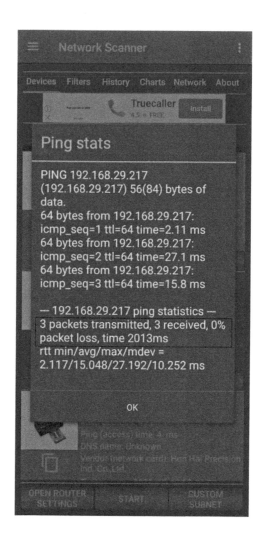

4. You can also check the ping of a particular device on your network. Ping usually checks the reachability to the target IP. It can check whether the specific target device is dead or alive. Click on the **PING STATS** button to check that device's ping statistics.

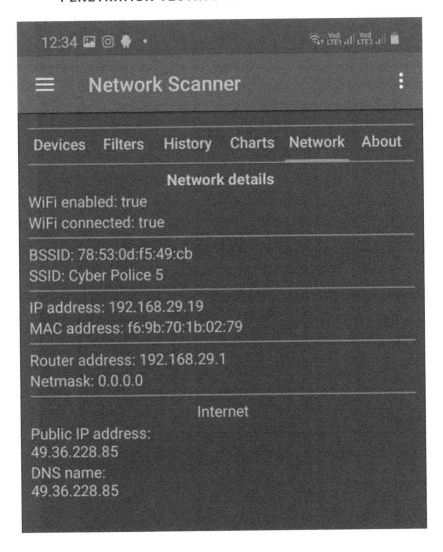

5. You can see many more details about your network by click-
ing on the network tab. It will show you the Router Address
(Private IP address of your router), Public IP address, DNS,
SSID, Private IP addresses and MAC addresses of your device.

Using Fing App to Find Open Ports

Fing app is a paid app, but many of its essential features are free to use.
   Fing app for Android: http://bit.ly/3jZWBQj
   Fing app for iOS: https://apple.co/2ZA1MQf

Using this app, you can also see the list of open ports. This way, you get an idea if your ports are correctly configured to your network/website. You can find out if any port is unnecessarily open for the intruder to find a loophole and intrude into your network/website by clicking on the **Find Open Ports**.

If no unnecessary port is open, it is an indication that your network/website is not vulnerable to any threats. Your pen-testing using a smartphone was successful. Enter the domain name (like tccsweb.com), and it will show all open ports on a website. Now, you can see that if unnecessary ports are opened, they can cause vulnerabilities. The list of open ports will be displayed something like (not exactly) as shown below:

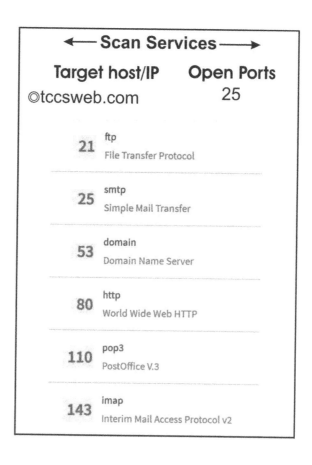

What Is a Port?

Let us understand the concept of ports from a real-life example. Suppose you prepare cookies for your friend and send your sibling to their house. To do this, he has to open the door of your home, then get out, then take the route to their defined address. Then your friend opens the door of their house and lets your sibling come inside. So, in the networking scenario, the cookie is the data you want to send, your brother is TCP/UDP connection, and the doors are the port numbers. When referring to a network or the Internet, software or network port is a location where information is sent. For example, port 80 is the HTTP network port.

Note: if you find unnecessary ports opened in your application, verify the *Nmap tool* to rule out false positives. You can also discuss the matter with your web developer so that as per services running, he can check the unnecessary opened ports.

Link to Similar Apps

Network Mapper (for Android)
Link: http://bit.ly/3bcgO1s
IP Network Scanner Lite (for iOS):
Link: http://apple.co/3qGd66Q

Conclusion

The readers have learnt about penetration testing and why it is required. They have understood how to test the network/website security using some smartphone apps. If a reader runs a company that involves electronic data and sensitive information, they can decide which kind of pen-testing is suitable for the company.

Multiple Choice Questions

1. When a pen-tester knows the complete network and other parameters, it is called:
   a. White-box pen-testing
   b. Black-box pen-testing
   c. Grey-box pen-testing
   d. None of the above

2. When a pen-tester has a partial knowledge network and other parameters, it is called:
   a. White-box pen-testing
   b. Black-box pen-testing
   c. Grey-box pen-testing
   d. None of the above

3. When you find more devices are connected to your Wi-Fi network than required, immediately what will be your next step?
   a. Change the Wi-Fi password
   b. Change the router's password
   c. Go outside and find intruders
   d. Call the police

4. When Ping is successful against a target IP that means:
   a. Target IP is dead
   b. Target IP is half-dead
   c. Target IP is Alive
   d. Target IP is unconscious

5. MAC address is a:

   a. Logical address of the device
   b. the physical address of the device
   c. The home address of the owner of the device
   d. The IP address of the device

ANSWER KEY

1	2	3	4	5
a	c	a	c	b

LAB TIME

1. Using the Network Scanner app, do the following:
   a. Find out how many devices are connected to your network. Observe results to check other details like private IP and MAC address of the devices.
   b. How will you come to know that no unauthorized device is connected to your IP?
   c. Ping various devices connected to your network using the Fing app.
2. Using the Fing app, look for open ports in a website. Also, look for devices connected to your Wi-Fi. Which additional features you observe in this app than the Network Mapper app.

16

P2P Money Transfer Apps and More

Case Study

Last week, Dilip Bhandari, 30, decided to put his mattress up for sale on an online platform for second-hand goods. Within hours, he was contacted by a man, Lakshman Singh, who claimed to be army personnel and expressed willingness to buy the mattress for ₹23,500. He then forwarded Bhandari a link to a Quick Response (QR) code and asked him to scan it so that he could transfer the money into his account.

Bhandari was a little puzzled by this mode of transaction but saw no harm as he wasn't giving out his bank details or other sensitive information. However, seconds after he scanned the QR code, he got a message that ₹10,000 had been debited from his account. He immediately called Singh, who apologized and said it was a mistake. He requested him to scan the code again, promising to wire the ₹10,000 along with ₹23,500 to his account.

"Bhandari scanned the code again only to see another ₹40,000 disappear from his bank account. When Bhandari tried to call Singh, his mobile phone was not reachable. He filed a complaint," said the police.

Reference: https://www.thehindu.com/news/national/karnataka/qr-code-scams-are-on-the-rise-in-city/article30239619.ece

These frauds can happen through any website selling mainly second-hand items, where people put their advertisements on these sites with descriptions and images of the product.

A buyer contacts the seller through the given portal as mediatory settles the deal and pays the money. Now comes the issue; the payment is usually made through payment apps called United Payment Interface (UPI) in India. So, in different countries, there can be other P2P apps like Zelle in the US, AliPay in China, TNG in Hong Kong, GoPay in Indonesia, Netspay in Singapore, etc.

Note: The Olx and other websites are mostly safe to use and do their best to protect users' privacy, and as soon as a suspicious user creates an

DOI: 10.1201/9781003148678-17

account or does some activity, they immediately flag it. But this world is big. People find different ways to defeat the security mechanism and create fake accounts to dupe sellers or become fictitious buyers.

Objectives

- To make secure payments through P2P fund transfer apps
- How can QR code be misused to fraud people?
- To protect yourself against online shopping frauds
  - To protect yourself against matrimonial/Romance frauds
- To learn about online shopping frauds
- To learn about matrimonial frauds

About Peer to Peer (P2P) Money Transfer Apps

United Payment Interface (UPI) apps in India like Google Pay, PhonePe and Paytm allow the transfer of money from one bank account to another instantly using one's mobile phone. These are peer-to-peer(P2P) apps. Payments can be made via an app on a mobile device only. For payment purposes, a Virtual Private Address (VPA) like 'soniarun1000@okhd-fcbank' is also generated.

One can pay another person by searching his mobile number (which is linked with their app), or entering the VPA or scanning the QR code generated by the app. One can also make a payment by entering the receiver's bank details (account number and IFSC code). These apps have quickly become favorites of both sellers and customers. Nowadays, most supermarkets and even street vendors have pasted the payment QR code at their places, and a customer needs to scan the QR code, enter the amount to be paid, click on the Pay button, enter the PIN and the payment will be made.

What Is a QR Code?

Now let us understand what a QR code is? To an ordinary person, a QR code is a matrix of black and white squares. But that is just like a curtain. What is hiding behind the curtain, you do not know. There can be proper programming (sometimes with malicious purpose) working behind this curtain.

This QR code is capable of many things. It can make you pay the money, direct you to a designated website (could be malicious too), make you save a contact in your phone and also capable of installing deadly malware in your phone. This deadly malware can hack all social media accounts on your phone, compromise bank account, read OTPs, access your contacts and much more.

Many payment apps and e-wallets have the feature of scanning a QR code for making payments easily.

What to Do to Avoid QR Code Frauds

The first line of action and protection is to avoid scanning a QR code. When some random person sends it to you to make the payments, there is a possibility that the QR code will have malicious programming behind it. Suppose the QR code is malicious; the money will be deducted from your account instead of deposited to your account. Or a deadly malware will get installed in your Smartphone, which will silently wipe out your savings from your account by compromising it. In short, anything can happen to whatever in your Smartphone.

Note: If the QR code is on a removable sticker even in a trusted shop, do not scan it.

Precautions to Take While Using These P2P Apps

These precautions are specifically for UPI apps in India but mainly applicable to all P2P money transfer apps worldwide.

1. Do not enter the PIN while receiving the money. Entering of PIN is required only in case of making the payment or checking your account balance

2. Always avoid scanning QR codes. If you have to make the payment, find that linked bank account through the mobile number. Ask the person to tell the phone number or the Virtual Private Address (VPA) like mine is soniarun1000@okhdfcbank for the Google Pay app, or bank account details to make the payment.

3. Never share your app PIN with anyone. Many survey forms request you to donate some money and cleverly ask you to enter your app PIN too.

4. If you get defrauded, do not look for support online. There are many cases where scammers have published fake websites to help you out with app issues. They will ask you to provide access to your Smartphone through remote administration tool apps (like Anydesk or team viewer). That way, they will take control and then access everything on your Smartphone. Always report the cybercrime in the cyber cell and use option (like Raise Dispute) in the app itself.

5. Always have a fingerprint scanning or strong PIN/password as your mobile phone lock. This lock is also going to secure your P2P app while using it to operate it.

6. The golden rule is, do not link your main bank account like a salary account with these P2P apps. Always maintain a separate bank account with less balance to connect with these apps. Because even after all the precautions, bad actors are coming with the latest methodologies for doing scams.

Online Shopping Frauds

In this Covid-19 pandemic the online shopping sky-rocketed. Almost everyone in the world who could afford to buy items of requirement used online shopping. But that also opened a plethora of opportunities for cybercriminals. A record number of malicious e-commerce web-sites mushroomed in just a matter of days. Those websites are still playing on the human psychology of "Greed" by providing 80% dis-count on expensive brands they successfully supplied the counterfeit material to customers. Some even merely took the order and never provided the ordered item. I still remember an incident where a per-son ordered an iPhone because the website gave a 60% discount on it. After two days, that person got a soap cake in the iPhone box.

Case Study

Many case studies on online shopping frauds can be read at:
https://timesofindia.indiatimes.com/topic/online-shopping-fraud
There is not a standard modus operandi for this type of cyber fraud. Online shopping fraud is the vastest winged cybercrime.

How to Safeguard Yourself

There are some precautions which you can take to secure yourself.

Know Them

It is easy to build an e-commerce website with an attractive name. You must confirm the physical address and landline number of the place. Do not shop through pop-ups that appear while you are browsing. For example, while you were searching the matter for your research paper, you suddenly get a pop-up asking you to shop Rolex watches at a 50% discount on a website. Do not rely on and follow-up such links. Legitimate companies do not attract buyers like this.

Compare the Deal

There are many websites which provide price comparison. For example, while buying an air ticket, you will get a price comparison of that route's air ticket from different airlines on many websites.

Keep Records

Always demand and save records of your online transaction. Product price, description, online receipt, and email communication between you and the seller should be carefully stored (preferably as a hard copy too, for a quick reference). It is possible that in your credit card statement, you find some additional charges by the seller which were not there when you ordered the item.

Read the Fine Prints

Check the privacy policy. You have the right to know how your personal information will be used. Suppose you cannot find a privacy policy, shift to some other website. Do read the refund policy too. It has happened in many cases after you ordered an item, the message "your order has been cancelled due to xyz reason, and you will get refund," appears but the refund never comes.

Free Trial?

Always be wary of free trials. The temptation (better say, greed) to try a product free for 15 days attract many customers. Here, you need to enter your credit card information to start the trial. Most of the times, you need to cancel the offer manually before the trial ends. Otherwise, the free trial will change into a full subscription/product.

Use Credit Cards to Make Purchases

Use credit cards to make purchases instead of debit cards. If your debit card details get stolen, it means the fraudster has direct access to your money in the bank account. The person can empty your bank account before you get any notification. But with a credit card, no one can directly touch the money in your bank account. The transaction will only be on your credit card, and the money won't be out of your bank account. You can quickly stop the transaction if you guess something is wrong. Many Mastercard and Visa cards, and all American Express cards, offer many types of protection (price, damage/theft) and extended warranty for their customers.

Matrimonial Frauds

There has been an exponential rise in Online Matrimonial (also romance) scams. The following case study will make things clear.

Case Study

NRI men, divorced, widowed women are easily falling as prey to matrimonial frauds. In one of the recent cases, a 44-year-old divorced woman was cheated by a Nigerian on an online matrimonial portal which she had joined last year, after being separated from her husband, The newspaper reports. "Fraudsters have been targeting women, who are in the age group of 35 to 50 years, and are either widowed or, divorced or looking for a partner on online matrimonial portals," the ACP explained. Not only women but NRI grooms too are falling into the trap of these community matrimony portals. In another case, a US-based man from Hyderabad was cheated of Rs 4 lakhs by a woman he wanted to marry after he met her on one of the online matrimony portals.

Source: https://iamcheated.indianmoney.com/news/matrimony-frauds-trap-nris-divorcees-and-widowers

If you explore the web, you will find thousands of cases where many women and men become a target for matrimonial fraud. And there is no stopping for that. Even there was one case where a woman cheated eight senior citizens on the pretext of marrying them, and then after a month, she used to elope with all the jewellery.

The Modus Operandi

The usual modus operandi is, fraudsters create exciting fake profiles on various matrimonial websites posing as software professionals or doctors or in any respectable profession, settled in foreign countries. They then start targeting persons, especially (but not necessarily) those looking for a second marriage. Then those fraudsters befriend persons of the opposite sex who show interest in their profiles.

They even use voice-changing apps to pose as parents and guardians of the bridegroom/groom when talking to the person they are trying to scam. Once they gain confidence, the fraudsters ask the other person to transfer money into their bank accounts, mentioning an emergency.

Even fraudsters go ahead of their limits, physically meet the other person, set a relationship with the other person, and then start blackmailing or getting money on some emergency pretext. And ultimately stop contacting the target and elope without leaving any trace behind.

How to Identify Fraudsters

- Most of the fraudsters create fake profiles and target opposite genders.
- They are reluctant to show their face in video conferencing or unwilling to meet in person.
- They express "love and feelings" quickly even before knowing each other well.
- They provide confused or inconsistent answers when asked for details of theirs or family
- Starts enquiring about your properties and income.

How to Safeguard Yourself

There are many steps that we can take to secure ourselves against matrimonial frauds

Always Visit a Reputed Matrimonial Website

Always go to a reputed matrimonial website to look for or to create your profile. There have been many cases where some matrimonial websites were part of the scam. Avoid using newly opened matrimonial websites. You can always check from www.whois.com launching date and other details about the website and its owner.

Always Look for Verified Profile Matches

Most of the reputed matrimonial websites have verified profiles. It means the verification experts have thoroughly checked those profiles, and you can trust those. So, look for a verified symbol on a profile before you progress.

Thorough Profile Check

Even you go for verified profiles, still do thorough research yourself on the person you want to marry. Start with their social media profiles. Look for any discrepancy in all social media accounts, like it is possible that address or working place could be different from where the person is claiming to live. Go to his working place to enquire about the person.

Be Cautious of Demand for Money

Do not transfer funds to prospective bridegroom or bride at any stage of conversation and under any circumstance. The moment someone asks you for money citing some reason, you avoid any further calls from them.

Stay Safe While Meeting in Person

While meeting the person in person, be cautious. It is advised that you meet in public places and inform your family about your meeting at the designated location.

Do Not Reveal Your Account Information

At any stage, avoid sharing any confidential information. It could be your social media account details or your bank account information. Once login details get shared, they can be misused in multiple ways against you. You can become a target of blackmailing and even become a cybercriminal in whose account illegally obtained money gets transferred. Also, avoid clicking on any link shared to you by another person in chat/messaging service or SMS.

Conclusion

Nobody is safe when it comes to money matters. From the websites selling second-hand goods, Online shopping and matrimonial commitments, all can become prey to cyber frauds. The only thing which can protect you is the knowledge of correct usage of technology and awareness. Even when one put one's property on rent, these scammers try to scam the person by the same methodology by agreeing to pay the advance rent. They do it by sending a QR Code or making the person enter incorrect bank details so that the money gets deducted from the account and credited to the bank account whose details the ignorant user has filled.

Multiple Choice Questions

1. To use an app like Google Pay, you need to have a laptop:
   a. Yes
   b. No
   c. Sometimes
   d. I do not know

2. You should safely scan all QR codes which are sent to you, even by unknown persons:
   a. Yes
   b. No
   c. I don't know!
   d. I told you, I don't know!

3. What is the safest way to transfer money through P2P banking apps (like UPI apps in India)?
   a. To transfer the amount using a person's mobile number
   b. To transfer amount using a person's VPA
   c. To transfer amount using a person's bank account number
   d. All of the above

4. Using which website one can know the inception date of a website?
   a. Whoami.com
   b. Whois.com
   c. Whatismyip.com
   d. Whatisdate.com

5. On a matrimonial website, what should you always look for?
   a. Handsome/beautiful faces
   b. Verified profiles
   c. Qualification
   d. Salary

ANSWER KEY

1	2	3	4	5
b	b	d	b	b

LAB TIME

1. Provide the name of any two P2P fund transfer apps in your country. Check the limit of the amount which can be transferred using those.

2. If some wrong/fraudulent transaction happens through some P2P app you use, how will you raise the dispute?

3. Find websites that can generate QR codes. Try to find the difference between static and dynamic QR codes. Generate a QR code that, when scanned, directs you to the Instagram profile - *arunsoni8182*. Scan that QR code and follow the account.

4. Read the terms and condition of your credit card for the situation if it is compromised and some illegitimate transactions happen.

17

FINAL THIRTY TIPS FOR ONLINE SAFETY

You have gone through the book and have read all chapters. Now it is time to sum-up all things. Moreover, there are many short and valuable points on which complete chapters cannot be created but are very important. Especially many apps and links which we can leverage to enhance our online safety. So here are some valuable tips, knowledge and a summary of what we have learnt, and what we missed too.

1. You often go to a cyber café or at some public place and use your USB drive to get printouts or for any other purpose. The data on your pen drive can get copied to the computer's hard disk (to which you attach your USB drive) without your knowledge and consent. Just imagine, along with one project file, you have 75 personal photographs. Your life can become disastrous if those photographs fall into the wrong hands.

DOI: 10.1201/9781003148678-18

Use email as a medium to open the file in a cyber café (or any public computer) and get the printout or for any other work. Otherwise, carry only the necessary file on your USB drive (not all your private photographs and other stuff). If there is a provision to save a file with a password (like MS Office documents), use it to protect it. Otherwise, create a password-protected zip file and then store it in the USB drive. Even if your file gets copied surreptitiously, the person cannot open it as the file is password-protected.

2. Someone can steal your login credentials by installing a keystroke recording software on a public computer or breaking your password using password-breaking tools. After this, that person can access your email/social media accounts and send objectionable emails/images from your account to your friends or unknown persons.

Set up 2-Factor Authentication offered by almost all email providers/ social media platforms to reduce the chance of being hacked. It will link your account with your smartphone. Whenever you have to log in, you must enter the verification code sent on your smartphone number along with the password. Many apps give you an option to use SMS or an authenticator app like Google Authenticator for this. Having 2-FA through Google Authenticator is more secure, as you need to download the app from the official app store, and it does not depend on the SIM card. So you are safe from SIM swap/cloning, through which the threat actor can hijack your SMS.

3. Suppose you click on a link that some unknown person sends through email or in a chat window. In that case, malware can infect your computer and record all your passwords and steal other information. That information can be misused and can cause mental stress and monetary loss to you. Are you curious to know some website that can check the link for maliciousness?

Always hover over the sender's name to see the actual URL from where it has arrived. If you think a URL is unsafe, you can use **www.virustotal. com** *to check for suspicious and malicious links. You can also use this website to check the integrity of a file before you open it(one another such website is* **www.jotti.org**). *These sites will review the submitted file by multiple genuine antiviruses free of cost.*

4. Suppose you do not secure the login details of your router. In that case, somebody can connect to your Internet, stop it, or even watch your online activities. It means all devices connected to your router can get compromised. Just understand, if you can open your router by using the default login (set by the manufacturer) details, anyone in the world can.

Do not forget to change the default (provided by the manufacturer) username and password of your router. Make sure to learn how to change your router's default password from the support person of the ISP (or someone you trust) and change it as soon as possible.

5. You can buy the world's best company's security camera, but those can get hacked if the default login details are not changed. The same goes for all IoT devices you install in your house.

Change the default login details just not for your router but every device you connect to your network. Many smart (IoT) devices are being used these days; all have a login panel, and you must change the default login credentials. Do read the manual of the connected device, learn about its configuration and default settings. If possible, connect your IoT devices to the Guest Wi-Fi network and not to the main Wi-Fi network.

6. When you open your email account or social networking site on a public computer, that page could be a phishing page. As you never know, someone could change the DNS settings in the router and instead of www.instagram.com, you will be displayed www.instagnam.com or similar

First of all, avoid using public computers. A public computer is that which is not your computer. Do not enter your login credentials in an already opened web page. Make sure you type the URL of the web page you want to access yourself in the browser's address bar. Even after the opening of the page, again check the URL for correctness. Wherever possible, use the virtual keyboard instead of the physical keyboard. That can save you from keyloggers.

7. If you are using a laptop, your device may be compromised without your knowledge, and somebody can be watching you through your webcam. It is also possible that your live streaming is being done on some objectionable website without your knowledge. Your webcam is taking

your pictures and are being emailed automatically to some bad actor.

Have a webcam cover to block the webcam of your laptop. If nothing else is available, use black tape to cover the lens (do not put it directly on the lens). If you are using an external webcam, disconnect it when not in use. While using the smartphone, install a camera blocker app like **"cameraless"** *to block the cameras. Whenever the use of the camera is required, you will be asked for permission. Smartphone camera covers are also available online.*

8. While surfing the web, if your web browser gives some warning about the web page's maliciousness, do not proceed further by ignoring it. These days browsers also give protection against malicious pages and unsecured web-site. Do not enter any type of information (filling forms, card details for online shopping) in HTTP://website. The information entered in such websites is not encrypted. Any bad actor in-between can read the entered data. That is why most of the browser shows the HTTP://website as "Insecure website."

Always enter information in websites starting from https://. These web-sites use another Secured Security Layer (SSL) for encryption and protection of data. These websites usually have a padlock icon in front of the website address.

9. Many times, hacking takes place because your Operating System, Antivirus and Web browser are not updated. It can happen because people use Pirated versions of OS or use free Antiviruses.

It is essential to keep your Browser, Operating system and Antivirus updated all the time because most of the updates consist of security patches. It is advised not to postpone or schedule the updates for later. Also, update all the apps you have installed when the update arrives.

10. A smartphone is our part of life. We download many types of apps in it. Always read reviews, check the rating and reputation of the developer before downloading any of them. Use

only official app stores (like Google Play Store for Android) to download apps. Even still, you cannot be sure about the maliciousness of the app. These official app stores can have malicious apps too.

Do not download any app through SMS or clicking on any external link. Check for permissions it is asking. If an app is asking for unnecessary permissions, do not download it. Always have a good legally purchased Antivirus on your phone. It can detect and warn you when a malicious app starts downloading on your smartphone.

11. We usually scan QR codes for many reasons, like to learn about a product (printed in newspaper advertisements), to make a payment or for any other cause like playing a video. These QR codes seem like a matrix of black and white squares. But these QR codes are programmed to perform some function (even a malicious one).

Avoid scanning any QR code sent by an anonymous person. Any such QR code can install the malware in your smartphone, redirect you to a malicious website or hack your phone to any extent. You cannot see which code is hiding behind the QR code. Dynamic QR codes are trackers too. The person in control of QR code can access information such as the scan's location, the number of scans, the time when the scans were performed, and the device's operating system.

12. Suppose you are using a P2P payment transfer app like United Payment Interface (UPI) apps in India (Google Pay, Bhim, PhonePe, and Paytm). Fraudsters send you a request for payment and at the same time ask you to enter the PIN.

Remember that you do not have to enter any PIN to receive the money. Entering of PIN is required when you make the payment or check your bank account balance. To make the payment using such apps, do not scan a QR code from an untrusted person. If you want to make a payment, search the person from his/her mobile phone number or ask the person to send the Virtual Private Address (VPA), not the QR code.

13. Sometimes you wonder how some of the data has even leaked out, or how come you see ads of something you just spoke about in a phone call. As these apps can talk to each other, and malicious apps can steal data from other apps, be careful about downloading apps.

Try to use the web browser to access your net banking and social media, as you will have an additional layer of security provided by the web browser. If you are using net banking from your phone, link an account with less money. Do not connect your main account (like your salary account) with it. With just one wrong click and your account can get compromised.

14. When you check how many devices are connected to your Wi-Fi using some app like Fing or Network Scanner, and found more than devices are at home, connecting to it. At that time, you need to change the Wi-Fi password. It is also possible that you want to do MAC filtering for the devices.

Learn to access the settings of your router. It is only possible when you know what the username and password of your router are. Most of the service providers do not give you this information while installing the router at your place. Make sure you ask for this information. Also, check the Wi-Fi encryption in Wireless settings (or some similar section) of your router. It should be WPA3 or WPA2 (WP2-PSK or WPA2-Personal in some settings). If the wireless router supports multiple wireless security protocols like WPA3, WPA2, WPA, you should use the most secure one, WPA3. WPA3 or WPA2 uses a more robust encryption algorithm, AES, that's very difficult to crack. Correct the encryption if you find it WEP or WPA.

Learn to set up a Guest Wi–Fi and isolate it from the main network. These days most modern routers have this feature. In case you have lots of friends or IoT devices, connect them to the Guest network so that if an IoT device or your friend's device gets compromised, your main network will not get affected. This option is best suited during Work From Home, as you can access your company's network from the main Wi–Fi and Gust network for other purposes. This is a simple way to regulate network segmentation between devices that you can control and have sensitive data on (such as your work laptop) and devices over which you have less control (like your smart lights).

15. Beware of social engineering attack by your known or even unknown ones. Social engineering is taking advantage of the goodness of people. Do not let any unauthorized person inspect or work on your PC. Even if a person visits your house/office claiming that he has been sent by a company for free servicing, can install a malware on your device.

There can be numerous examples and case studies where people easily gave away sensitive information of the office/house to bad actors after falling prey to their social engineering tricks. Always be alert and do not provide your sensitive information to anyone on any pretext. Always give your PC/smartphone for repair to a trusted and the company's authorized person. Always check the identity card of the person who comes to the house to repair your devices.

16. Email accounts are often broken into, so don't trust them to store your passwords. Neither it is advisable to maintain a diary to write you passwords. It becomes cumbersome when you update your passwords, or you might lose your diary on some lousy day.

Use password managers to store and manage user names and passwords of your accounts. These password managers can keep as well as generate strong passwords for you. After entering login details for all your accounts in a password manager, you can also take a printout of all of your account's login credentials. Not only login-details of email/social media accounts, but details of all your credit/debit cards can also be stored in it and never lost.

17. Open public Wi-Fi networks are notorious for exposing people's personal information to anyone. The Man-In-The-Middle

(MITM) attack can leak your information in transit to any bad actor in-between.

Avoid getting connected to Free Internet Wi-Fi access zones. If you want to access information through a free-Wi-Fi, always use a Virtual Private Network(VPN) to access the web. Choose a VPN that has AI integrated and a no-log policy.

18. An unattended ATM has high chances of having skimmers installed on it. When you swipe your card at gas stations or restaurants again, the chances are that the card will get cloned.

Try to use an ATM that is inside a bank or guarded 24 hrs by some bank guard. Use EMV chip-based NFC cards which are without any magnetic stripe. These cards are almost impossible to clone. Some countries are still providing cards with a magnetic strip. Tell your bank to replace those with EMV Chip cards.

19. Many times you will see that some new e-commerce websites are giving a huge discount on products. Always suspect an unbelievable discount. Also, suspect a new online shopping website which is not very popular.

Check the year of inception of that website on www.whois.com. *Always rely on trusted and older online shopping websites. Do not save your credit card details on the shopping websites, as if their infrastructure gets compromised, the details of your card may get into the wrong hands. Use only HTTPS://websites to enter the details of your card.*

20. If you lose your card, even a person who finds it and does not know the PIN can use it for online shopping. Generally,

while using a credit/debit card online, you need to enter some details like card no., validity month/year, three digits Card Verification Value (CVV) number. All these details are present on the card. So there remains the possibility that before you report the lost card, someone can use it for online shopping, and you will get a hefty bill sent to your address.

You can erase the CVV number on the card after remembering it or note it down somewhere else. So that even when you lose the card somehow, no online transaction can be done using it. Always inform the card provider bank in case of the change of mobile number, address or any detail. Do not depend on an OTP to come on your registered mobile number after an online transaction. This OTP rule varies from country to country.

21. We usually have a paper statement for our credit/debit card or extra photocopies of the Aadhar card (India), Social security card (US), etc., in our house. When you want to throw those away, destroy them properly. Make sure that nobody can pick it up from the garbage bin (in hacking, it is termed as "Dumpster Diving") and can misuse it.

If possible, stop having paper statements for your card. Be in the habit of reading card statements online or through email. Some bad actors can use details from these carelessly thrown papers to rent an apartment, take a bank loan, or for any other malicious purpose. Also use https://www.fileshredder.org/ *to delete the files so that those become irrecoverable. Otherwise, simply deleting and emptying the recycle Bin is not sufficient.*

22. Don't provide a photocopy of both sides of the card to anyone. It is like giving a copy of the card to anybody. In case you lose the card, inform the bank immediately. Banks can block and prevent the misuse of the card.

Do read the policy of the bank related to your card. By giving immediate information to the bank about the loss of the card within the stipulated time, you will not lose the money even when an illegal transaction has been done.

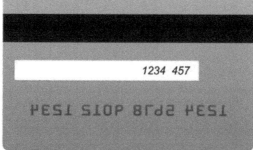

23. Your card or card details can be stolen anytime by some bad actor. And the person can do illegal transactions on that. Are there any more security measures you can take?

That is why many card companies provide extra security (like Mastercard Securecode or Verified by Visa). It will allow you to create an additional password which only you know. For example, MasterCard SecureCode is a private code for your MasterCard account that gives you an extra layer of online shopping security. Only you and your financial institution know what your code is – retailers aren't able to see it. So you can trust that your transactions get independent approval every time.

24. A bad actor can set a rogue hot-spot point (with the same SSID and Password). Innocent users will automatically get connected to it because of its strong signal. Now the person can impersonate your identity and take control of the session. This is the 'Evil Twin' method of MITM attack.

Always use a public Wi-Fi through a VPN. A VPN provides an encrypted tunnel to your data. That way, no one (ISP, hacker or even government) can see what you are accessing.

25. **Smartphones are expensive and contain a lot of information about us, maybe social or financial. If stolen or misplaced, someone can play havoc with our lives.**

Always have a biometric or PIN-based lock to access your phone. While using your smartphone to do banking transactions, log out after the transaction is complete. Also, install some security software (like the Prey app) and know how to operate an in-built tracking feature (like "Find my Mobile" in Android and "Find my iPhone" in iOS). So that if you lose your mobile, you can track it, lock or wipe out your mobile data remotely.

26. We are always worried about our close ones' emergencies. Especially for women and elderly ones when they have gone away from home. Where are they? Are they safe? And lots of other things keep coming to our mind.

You can have a tracking app for your close ones linked to your mobile phone. When the SOS button on their phone is activated (by clicking or even screaming), the app will send a notification alert and his/her current location to specified contacts. Define a safe zone in the app for your close ones so that you get notified when your close one(s) go out of the safe zone. For example, you can set the nearest market or the area until your child's tuition center as a safe zone. Whenever your child steps out of that safe zone, you will get notified.

27. Whatever we browse, the browser saves our browsing history within it. Anyone can view that browsing history. Using the incognito mode on Chrome browser (or Private window in Firefox browser) on a shared computer will stop others from seeing your browsing history. But being the anonymous effect is at the local level only. It means your ISP can still see what you are doing. In fact, on a mobile phone, it can see which app and which URL you have typed and send data to advertisers. Of course, he might be getting a commission for that.

Use a privacy-oriented browser like Tor Browser, Brave Browser or Epic Browser and use a privacy-oriented Search engine like DuckDuckGo, which do not track you. Moreover, whichever browser you use, keep it updated. An up-to-date browser keeps your computer secure, protecting you from many types of cyberattacks like identity theft, phishing attacks, viruses, trojans, spyware, adware, and other sorts of malware. Again we recommend use of a VPN while browsing the sensitive information.

28. In many countries, people buy pirated Windows OS for less than ten US dollars. Buying pirated software is the norm there. Even many messaging apps sell such software through their groups/channels.

Such software is mainly pre-activated with Virus, Trojan or Spyware and will take control of your computer. Whatever you are doing will be passed on to some third party. There is no doubt that legal software is expensive. But once purchased, it can save you from lots of troubles like piracy and malware. You will be able to update the legally purchased software that will protect you from lots of cyberattacks.

29. Never underestimate the importance of backup. May things we do not realize till we lose them. The same goes for the backup too. Ransomware can strike anytime and to anyone. It will encrypt your data and make it inaccessible to you until you pay the ransom amount. Even then, there is no guarantee that your data will be released.

If you have the backup, you can restore it on a new computer or after formatting the same computer. Always have an offline backup, too, because the Ransomware can take control of all connected drives.

30. Let us modify the above situation. Imagine the situation that some bad actor has taken control of your data through some ransomware and is threatening to send captured data to your competitors. Then even backup cannot save you.

So here comes the part of learning to encrypt your data. It means once you encrypt your data using utilities like BitLocker (inbuilt in Windows 10) and VeraCrypt (You can download and use it for free). By encrypting, data becomes unreadable. Only you can decrypt it to make it readable. Now even some bad actor captures your data on the hard drive; it will be useless for him/her as it is encrypted and in an unreadable form. You should be aware that cryptography is the study of ideas such as encryption, whereas encryption is a technique for concealing messages through the use of algorithms.

The message is converted from plaintext to ciphertext by the sender. Encryption is the term for this portion of the procedure. The cipher-text is sent to the recipient. The ciphertext message is converted back to plaintext by the receiver. This part of the process is called decryption. Digital signatures, which provide an assurance of message integrity, use encryption techniques. Encrypted data is commonly referred to as ciphertext, while unencrypted data is called plaintext.

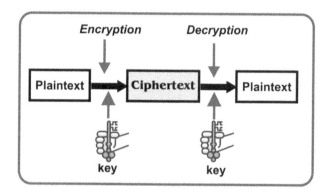

Note: Perhaps one of the oldest practical use of cryptography was implemented by the Romans in the Caesars Cipher. The technique, also known as shifting cipher, replaces each character of the language with a character of fixed length distance from it, the distance being called the shift. For English language the shift of 3 would mean the cipher mapping becoming as shown in the figure below.

PlainText	A	B	C	D	E	F	G	H	
CIpherText	D	E	F	G	H	I	J	K	

The cipher above will change a given sentence as follows:

Plain Message: I AM A GOOD GIRL

Cipher Text: H DP D JRRG JLUO

18

REPORTING A CYBERCRIME

Scenario

You were searching for the helpline number of a website through which you bought an Air Ticket. After making the payment successfully, you just received the booking ID number but not a copy of the ticket. You searched for the Portal's customer care number and dialed the one which appeared in the search.

The executive picked up the phone and told you that the ticket was not booked and would initiate a refund. For that, he requires your bank details so that he can transfer the refund money to your account. Then you received an OTP, and the executive asked you to share that same with him. He assured you that the refund would be processed immediately, and the amount will be transferred to your bank account. But as you shared the OTP, a large amount got deducted from your bank account. And then you realized that you had become a victim of cybercrime.

Also, at the same time, you realized that you do not know where to report the cybercrime. You also did not know that you should have saved (exported) the WhatsApp chat which you had with that customer care executive to be produced as digital evidence. You did not know how to do that. You also did not realize that you should have also saved the URL of the fake customer care website.

Objectives

- Essentials for reporting a cybercrime
- Reporting cybercrime all over the world

Introduction

Cybercrime is borderless. The evidence can be removed very fast. For example, someone sent you an objectionable message on WhatsApp

DOI: 10.1201/9781003148678-19

199

but deleted it immediately after you have read it. It will become difficult for you to produce that message as a piece of evidence since you did not take a screenshot of that (or did not know how to save the whole chat). Moreover, delay in reporting can help cybercriminal to remove his/her tracks.

Reporting a Cybercrime

These days, newspapers are full of cases of all types of cybercrimes like hacking, cyberstalking, revenge porn, sextortion, financial frauds, DDoS attack, Online scams (Lottery/Job/Romance), Ransomware and a lot more. It can strike anytime due to its global nature. One should always be ready to face it and report it immediately if, unfortunately, it happens to you.

Each country has an online method to report cybercrime (like in India, it is www.cybercrime.gov.in). It will help if you have email IDs/hotline and phone numbers of cybercrime officials related to your area with you. So, we are guiding you on how to approach the same.

1. In the case of cybercrime, the victim should try to preserve and download all the evidence essential to file a complaint. Evidences may include: Credit card receipt, Bank statement, Online money transfer receipt, copy of email, URL of the webpage, Chat transcripts, saved videos and images.
2. The victim can contact the nearest police station and lodge a formal complaint with the local police. The local police will either guide or hand over the case to cyber cell (Internet Police). The victim will be contacted in due time by the authorities.

Most countries have dedicated online portals for reporting cyber-crime. For some countries, cybercrime can be reported by emailing the complaint to the Internet Police or by lodging a complaint through the link given on the local police website or cybercrime cell website.

The challenge for a victim is to find the email ID of the cyber cell or the cybercrime portal to report the crime. We have researched to provide readers the available links for the cybercrime cell (Internet police) website of different countries.

Link to Cybercrime Cells/Portals (Internet Police) Websites

India: www.cybercrime.org.in
   USA: https://www.ic3.gov/
   Canada: https://www.rcmp-grc.gc.ca/
   Australia: https://www.cyber.gov.au/acsc/report
   UK: https://www.actionfraud.police.uk/
   New Zealand: https://www.police.govt.nz/105support
   UAE: https://www.dubaipolice.gov.ae/wps/portal/home/services/individualservicescontent/cybercrime (Short link: http://bit.ly/UAE-Cyber-reporting)

For other countries, links to cybercrime portals are available on this web page: http://www.ccmostwanted.com/report-cybercrime-worldwide/ (Short link: http://bit.ly/worldwide-reporting)

Note: We have tried our best to gather information on cybercrime cells from various sources. Still, it is advised that readers should verify the authority on his/her behalf.

Further Reading

S.NO.	ABOUT	URL	QR CODES
1	Various types of Hackers	https://www.jigsawacademy. com/blogs/cyber-security/ different-types-of-hackers/	

2	Various types of malware, with examples	https://www.crowdstrike.com/ cybersecurity-101/malware/ types-of-malware/	
3	How to Make a Career in Ethical Hacking?	https://www.geeksforgeeks.org/ how-to-make-a-career-in- ethical-hacking/	
4	Various Certifications in Ethical Hacking	https://www.testpreptraining. com/blog/ ethical-hacking-certifications/	
5	Cybersecurity Careers	https://www. cybersecurityeducation.org/ careers/	

	USEFUL WEBSITES	PURPOSE
1	https://www.virustotal.com/	This website analyzes suspicious files and URLs with more than 50 types of antiviruses to detect malware.
2	https://virusscan.jotti.org/	This site is similar to virustotal.com but can scan only files which you submit to it.
3	https://web.archive.org/	The Wayback Machine is a digital archive of the WWW. It allows the user to go to a specific date and view what websites looked like in the past. A user can also extract the old information from there.
4	www.yougetsignal.com	YouGetSignal is a collection of uncomplicated, powerful network tools like port scanners, reverse IP lookups, reverse Domain lookups, WHOIS lookups, etc.
5	www.whois.com	Whois Domain Name & IP lookup service to search the whois database for verified registration information.
6	www.fotoforensics.com	FotoForensics provides tools and training for digital picture analysis, including error level analysis, metadata and tutorials.

7	https://unshorten.it/	Unshorten.it is a URL unshortner that lets you know the actual link behind a shortened URL. It is possible that a malicious link is there behind the shortened URL, so always unshorten it to see what is hiding behind.
8	https://www.webcrawler.com	It is a web crawler search engine that crawls the web very quickly to provide you with all the related results to the target that is searched in the query box.
9	https://osintframework.com/	OSINT framework can be used to gather information from free tools or resources. You will find many Open Source INTelligence (OSINT) tools.
10	https://howsecureismypassword.net/	A website to test the strength of your password.
11	https://haveibeenpwned.com/	A website to check, has your email id been compromised in a data breach? It will also notify you if your email gets compromised in a future breach.
12	https://urlscan.io/	URLScan.io is a website scanner. It can analyze all possible details about the website. It also finds and analyzes malicious websites and phishing too. Explore it!

	USEFUL CHROME EXTENSION	PURPOSE
1	Nimbus	To help to collect the digital evidence.
2	Hunter.io	To find professional email addresses.
3	Wappalyzer	Helps in performing website fingerprinting. You can get detail of all technologies used to develop a website.
4	Open port check tool	With the Open Port Check Tool, a user can easily identify open ports that are not in use (even remotely). You can also get a list of DNS server, which will reduce your DNS lookup time, and it may speed up your browsing experience. Also, family safe DNS servers can be found.
5	Privacy Badger	No one wants to be tracked while making any financial or any other transactions. Privacy Badger automatically blocks invisible trackers.
6	Adblock	Adblock extension automatically blocks annoying ads on the websites you visit. It also protects your browser from malware and stops advertisers from accessing your browsing history and personal information.
7	Setup VPN	It is a lifetime free VPN.
8	snov.io	It is an email finder extension. It also helps in Gmail to find whether the receiver has opened the sent email or not.
9	inVid	This extension exposes fake news and verifies images and videos forensically.
10	Polarr Photo Editor	Using this extension, one can professionally edit any photo on the internet with one click.

Index